12-10-76

Living with people at home or at work is not easy. Many interpersonal relationships often result in misunderstandings, or even hostility. In Dr. Hyder's first book, THE CHRISTIAN'S HANDBOOK OF PSYCHIATRY, he gave many answers to frequently asked questions, and many solutions to problems in these areas. He competently fused together fundamental psychological theories with basic Christian principles. THE PEOPLE YOU LIVE WITH forms a sequel to the HANDBOOK and concisely offers some suggestions as to how to get along better with the people with whom you are presently living or working. By integrating biblical principles with his professional training as a psychiatrist, he clearly deals with the various stages involved in personality development and the many problems which arise during those and later years.

Blending the elements of common sense, sound psychological theory, and a profound personal faith in Christ as Saviour and Lord, he confronts the issues that threaten the stability and harmony of modern family life—child discipline, teen-age identity crises, unwed mothers, communication between family members, in-laws, sexual problems in and out of marriage, adultery, old age, and dying—and responds to them with practical, dynamic, Christ-centered principles of living.

Dr. Hyder's wise perception and discernment of human problems allow him to offer expert advice for understanding the reality of a situation, how to become more responsible in it, and the resources available to every Christian for freedom and healing. The committed Christian is challenged to seek a deeper relationship with his Lord and to improve his human relationships. The person seeking mental health is persuaded to consider more responsibly the various alternatives open to him. To all of us,

(Continued on back flap)

(Continued from front flap)

he gives hope that our situation is curable; that we can change by the grace of God if we really want to; and that life has meaning and purpose if seen through the eyes of our Creator.

What hangs us up is ourselves. THE PEOPLE YOU LIVE WITH attempts to show us how we can be set free from ourselves— our own worst enemies—and live in peace with others and with God. Psychotherapy has its place in helping to mold a person into a whole being—body, mind and spirit. God, who knows us the best because He made us, has said some very timely and significant things in His Word that we need to absorb diligently and apply to ourselves personally. This book integrates, in a language easily understood by a layman, the discipline of psychotherapy with the discipline of being a follower of Jesus in the everyday routine of relating to people.

Being a disciple of Jesus is not easy, nor is living with people. Even being a "new creation in Christ" does not rid us of problems and sin overnight. Jesus, reigning in our hearts, gives us insight into our problems, power to change our habitual behavioral patterns, and freedom from our self centeredness. He also gives us a new wi united with His will, which embraces inn peace, joy, true freedom, a knowledge of truth, and a committed love for others.

After reading THE PEOPLE YOU WITH you might just find that some pe will want to live with you!

THE PEOPLE YOU LIVE WITH

O. QUENTIN HYDER, M.D.

FLEMING H. REVELL COMPANY
Old Tappan, New Jersey

Scripture quotations not otherwise identified are from the King James Version of the Bible.

Scripture quotations identified NEB are from The New English Bible. © The Delegates of the Oxford University Press and the Syndics of the Cambridge University Press 1961 and 1970. Reprinted by permission.

Scripture quotations identified MOFFATT are from THE BIBLE: A NEW TRANSLATION by James Moffatt. Copyright 1954 by James A. R. Moffatt. By permission of Harper & Row, Publishers, Inc.

Portion of the poem "The Ladies" from RUDYARD KIPLING'S VERSE: Definitive Edition. Reprinted by permission of Mrs. George Bambridge and Doubleday & Company, Inc.

Library of Congress Cataloging in Publication Data

Hyder, O Quentin, date
    The people you live with.

    Bibliography: p.
    1. Marriage. 2. Family. Conduct of life.
I. Title.
HQ734.H97   261.8′34′2   74-32317
ISBN 0-8007-0697-8

TO
the people I have lived with:
my father, mother, and sister
and
my wife, daughter, and son

CONTENTS

Preface   9

Acknowledgments   13

PART I

The Personal Christian Life

1 Principles of Healing   19
2 Mind, Emotions, and Will in the Christian Experience   31
3 Psychological Defense Mechanisms   42

PART II

The Family

4 Early Development and Adult Regression   59
5 Some Principles of Raising Young Children   71
6 Unwed Pregnancy and Other Problems of Adolescence   81

PART III

Youth

7   Emotional Problems of Youth   95
8   Social Problems of Youth   106
9   Sexual Problems of Youth   115

PART IV

Christian Marriage

10   Choice and Temperament in Marriage   135
11   Finances and Communication in Marriage   146
12   Sexual Problems in Marriage   154
13   Infidelity and Divorce   163

PART V

Declining Years

14   Aging and Dying   179

     Suggested Reading   191

PREFACE

After the publication of my first book *The Christian's Handbook of Psychiatry* in 1971, many of my Christian friends asked me to expand on several ideas contained in it. This book, four years later, forms a sequel, giving several practical applications to many of the theoretical concepts previously presented. It is based on my experiences as a Christian counselor and physician of twenty years, the last ten of which have been as a psychiatrist.

No man can experience personally all the problems and difficulties about which he writes. I have experienced some—I have been depressed; I have been anxious; I have been lonely; I have experienced guilt and forgiveness; I have suffered personal and professional failure. I have also enjoyed the thrill and satisfaction of success. I know what it is like to remain single into one's late thirties, and to continue to study for professional qualifications well into middle age. I am learning the meaning of the word *wait* in God's dealings with His people. On the brighter side, I also know the joy of a happy marriage to the woman whom God in His perfect wisdom and love had prepared for me. I had to wait long for her because in order to prepare *me* for *her*, God had to do a lot of work in me first. I know the joy of having a young daughter and son and am excited about the years ahead in which we will all grow and learn together as a family centered in Christ.

Beyond learning from these experiences in my own life, I have gained much from talking with others: my patients, friends, and professional colleagues. The chapters that follow expound some ideas I have formulated in the last two decades. Most of these are based on the experience of dealing with the problems of those who have come to seek my advice as a psychiatrist and Christian counselor. The majority of my patients have come not because they have been mentally ill, but because they have been disappointed in their interpersonal relationships, such as between husbands and wives, or parents and children. Many have suffered failures in life's major arenas such as school, dating, sex life, career, raising a family, social encounters, or getting along with other Christians in the church. Other ideas stem from my own spiritual experiences as a Christian pilgrim, enduring defeats yet also glorifying in God-given victories in this lifelong struggle to yield and be faithful to my divine Guide.

This book, unlike the previous one, is not intended mainly for pastors, counselors, or mature Christians seeking to help others with personal problems—it is directed toward those actually walking through those problems. Scores of situations which arise throughout life—in childhood, youth, courtship, family, job, and old age—are considered in depth. This book is written for the nonprofessional, for the believing Christian layman, trying to live up to his or her profession of faith, but struggling with internal or interpersonal-relationship problems. Although the book is written by a physician, it can be read and understood by anyone without a scientific education or technical knowledge. Psychiatric or other technical words used are either explained, or their meaning is readily apparent from the context. The chapters can be read in any order and the reader is encouraged to go first to those whose titles seem to interest him most.

My prayer is that *The People You Live With* may help many Christians better to understand themselves and their loved ones. If a few families will become happier, and a few Christians will live closer to Jesus after prayerfully reading it, then my efforts in writing the book will have been worthwhile.

O. QUENTIN HYDER

ACKNOWLEDGMENTS

Reading between the lines in this book you can tell that I have been profoundly influenced not only by my professional training, but also by the experiences of striving to live the Christian life for the last twenty-five years. I have shared, I think, somewhat more of myself in this book than most author-psychiatrists are willing to do. This is because I want to give back to others that which I have received from God and from my friends—Christian and non-Christian. My present character and personality are very much the products of those who have influenced me throughout my forty-five years in this life.

Preeminent among these are my parents, Dr. Roland I. Hyder and Dr. Louise S. Hobbs, of Ipswich, England, who gave to me and my sister Valerie a good home, careful upbringing, first-class education, and most important, a solid foundation in moral principles, personal integrity and a determination to achieve professional competence. Yet at the same time our family was able to relax and enjoy ourselves in wholesome ways. Two other physicians more recently have helped me greatly both in my professional career and also personally. They are Professor Lawrence C. Kolb, Chairman of the Department of Psychiatry, College of Physicians and Surgeons, Columbia University; and Dr. Ronald Fieve, Professor of Internal Medicine at the New York State Psychiatric Institute, Columbia-Presbyterian Medical Center of New York City.

I also owe a lot to my patients. I see an average of fifty people each week, and over the years the notes I have made from our many thousands of hours of dialogue have contributed immeasurably to some of the ideas and opinions expressed herein.

Many Christian friends have been a special source of blessing and guidance to me. Outstanding among these have been Dr. Stephen F. Olford, one of the greatest preachers in America today and Pastor Emeritus of the Calvary Baptist Church in New York City, who has honored me several times with invitations to share with him in his "Encounter" television programs; Rev. Jim DiRaddo, co-director with me at the Christian Counselling and Psychotherapy Center, without whose enthusiasm our Center might never have become a reality; and Miss Allison Brown, Jim's and my secretary, who thoroughly scoured my original manuscript and insisted on countless changes and additions which have vastly improved the final result. I am grateful also to the dedicated Christian ladies who did all the typing for me: Mrs. Elizabeth Brooks, Mrs. Linda Sava Jackson, Miss Ruth Munsinger, and Miss Millie Zarco.

Finally I acknowledge my indebtedness to my loving wife, Lou-Ann. She patiently, with selfless understanding, accepted the deprivation of time that this writing took—time that would otherwise have been given to her. She has also taught me a lot about myself; and many of the thoughts expressed in this book stem from her contributions to our happy and fulfilling marriage, home, and family.

O. QUENTIN HYDER

THE PEOPLE YOU LIVE WITH

PART I

The Personal Christian Life

1

....

PRINCIPLES OF HEALING

Many of my professional colleagues are sceptical about the attempts being made by several psychiatrists (including myself) who are committed Christian believers, to bring biblical principles into the techniques of psychotherapy. Though in a minority, there are approximately a hundred fully trained psychiatrists in this country who are also committed evangelical Christians. There are also many clinical psychologists, professional counselors, and certified social workers, licensed to practice psychotherapy, who profess Christ as Saviour and Lord, and who embrace a conservative Protestant theology. Add to these a number of devout Roman Catholic practitioners of various trainings and backgrounds who sincerely attempt to counsel or practice psychotherapy within the general precepts of Christian doctrine. All these men and women, located all over this country and the rest of the world, are making their voices heard.

Psychoanalysis and psychotherapy have far too long been influenced by atheism or agnosticism. In spite of statements to the contrary, it is inevitable that an analyst's own philosophical and religious views will influence his therapy. So many moral issues arise in a course of treatment that no therapist can avoid his own beliefs and prejudices affecting both the comments he makes and also the leading questions he asks.

Though a therapist may claim that he is neutral or nonreligious, if he says anything to a patient which is contrary to the patient's own personal belief system he is in fact having a religious influence.

This might not always be bad, indeed it could be helpful to the patient, but the fact remains that it is a definite influence on his beliefs. The resultant image, therefore, of psychiatrists and psychologists in the minds of many devout Christians has been that we are instruments of the devil, his latest method of implanting doubt and of undermining the peace and security of the faithful.

My task in both my first book and this one is to help reverse this trend. I am writing as a trained and experienced psychotherapist who totally submits to the authority of the Holy Scriptures. Further, I attempt to combine biblical teachings, whenever beneficial, with all the different forms of therapy needed by patients, whether they be directive, supportive, behavorial, nondirective, or analytic. I make no attempt whatever to hide or deny my own prejudices. Unlike the nonreligious, I admit my beliefs. More, I attempt to integrate them with my therapy whenever I believe it will be appropriate and helpful to the patient. I am more free to be directive than most therapists because it is not my authority but that of the Word of God that I use as my guide and foundation.

This book, however, is not a technical textbook. It is not written for my fellow therapists and counselors but for men and women like the hundreds I have been privileged to help in the last several years. It is not a do-it-yourself, quick cure-all for personal and family problems. It is written specifically to help the intelligent Christian layman to understand more about himself, his needs, and his relationships.

Over the main entrance to the Presbyterian Hospital in Manhattan are these words: "For of the Most High Cometh Healing." The expression, "I treat, God heals," is attributed both to Ambroise Paré, sixteenth-century French military surgeon and also to Sir William Osler, the great Oxford physician and teacher of the early 1900s. All our efforts as physicians would be in vain if our God-created bodies did not have within them the ability to heal themselves and to resist and reverse disease processes. ". . . for I am the Lord that healeth thee" (Exodus 15:26). All healing of physical disorders, whether natural or supernatural, comes ultimately from God. He alone defines and delivers health. Healing therefore, is partially a mystery to us. Some are cured, others are not. God holds the key and we find peace as we accept His omnipotent providence.

Though not so obvious, I submit that these truths are equally valid in the case of mental or emotional illnesses. The situation is complicated by the fact that unlike physical or organic illnesses, mental and emotional problems are usually at least partially within the patient's conscious control. The *will* is involved, and this leads to complications when motivation for change is inadequate. In psychiatric practice, therefore, we have to say, "I treat, God heals if the patient wants Him to." The element of individual responsibility on the part of the sufferer is an integral part of his therapy. The Lord's question, "Wilt thou be made whole?" (*see* John 5:6) is more pertinent in psychiatric practice than in any other branch of medicine. In general medical and surgical illnesses most patients need only to make a single decision, that of yielding themselves in trust to their doctor's advice with regard to the treatment plan for their particular problems. However, in problems affecting mood and behavior, responsible, well-motivated cooperation by the patient is needed constantly day by day, hour by hour. If the outworkings of psychotherapy in the form of positive practical changes are to be seen in the daily life of the sufferer, he has to be constantly on guard against relapse into the old, easier behavior patterns. Psychotherapy, be it analytic, supportive, or directive can only expect to achieve in the patient a deeper self-understanding and a knowledge of what changes he needs to put into effect. Unwillingness to follow through is a moral or spiritual hindrance. The exercise of the will is an integral part of healing. The patient is responsible to cooperate in therapy by doing all he can, within his understood and agreed emotional limits, to effect the necessary changes within himself that healing requires.

With the possible sole exception of serious psychotic loss of reality contact, the patient usually retains some measure of voluntary control. There is a growing increase in psychiatric opinion that serious reality-contact loss is caused by some chemical imbalance, as evidenced, for example, by the similarity between psychosis and the subjective experiences of an LSD trip, and also by the fact that the introduction of other chemicals such as the phenothiazines can significantly reduce psychotic symptoms. It is *after* the psychotic has returned to reality that psychotherapy can be of help to him.

This fact applies equally to psychotherapy practiced within a biblical framework by a therapist who is a Christian believer. Distressed relatives of a Christian who is undergoing a serious breakdown need to be reassured that even though the doctors in the hospital might not be believers, they can be trusted to effect with medications the chemical healing that is initially essential. Once reality contact has been restored, a Christian therapist can be sought for ongoing outpatient treatment.

Assuming that a patient is not psychotic and is motivated to change, we come now to consider psychotherapeutic principles of healing within a biblical framework. I call this *Christian Psychotherapy* which I regard in my own hands as a definite technique, not simply therapy practiced by someone who happens to call himself a Christian. It involves a biblical view of God, man, sin, and redemption. Salvation and santification are parts of the healing process. Repentance always precedes restoration to health and peace.

Psychiatry is still in its infancy. We hear today of psychoanalysis, primal therapy, transactional analysis, behavior therapy, rational therapy, and a host of other theories which may or may not be of practical value in treatment. All of these divergent ideas merely reflect the obvious fact that psychiatrists and psychologists are groping and exploring, seeking to find more effective ways of helping the pained and distraught people who put their trust in them for help. It is said that George Washington was bled to death by his physicians because in those days bloodletting was considered good treatment for the pneumonia from which he was suffering. We know better now, but psychiatrists today are experimenting in the same way as their medical colleagues were doing two hundred years ago. We have to try new approaches: to keep and use that which works and to abandon that which fails or proves harmful. We also have the obligation to keep in touch with medical and psychiatric research by being up to date with reading our professional literature.

As Christian therapists we have an additional resource which is not new. In the pages of Holy Scripture are hundreds of verses which can be of value in the process of Christian psychotherapy. The Bible is man's God-given handbook for living according to His will. It reveals the truth about man to himself. Though morally and spiritually very complex, man is knowable through humble searching of God's Word. It is the responsibility of the Christian therapist to be sufficiently familiar with the Bible so that he can apply verses from it whenever appropriate, either by quoting or showing them to his patient. There is also the resource of prayer, both for and with the patient. In such needs as elevation of depressive mood, reduction of internal stress, and alleviation of anxiety, I have found spoken prayer at the end of a session extremely therapeutic.

This raises another matter in the whole area of the principles of healing. Therapy is not only a technique—it is a relationship. It is a relationship between a patient and his doctor. It is also a relationship between an anxious inquirer and his Christian counselor. This puts great responsibility upon the counselor or therapist. He must be professionally competent, thoroughly trained and skillful through experience, free from personal hang-ups, and above reproach in his exemplary private life-style and professional decorum. Many Christians who come as patients have already been to their pastors and have prayed about their problems. They go to a professional counselor as a last resort, often prepared to accept what he says as God's will for their lives. The office of the Christian therapist then becomes not only a place for professional healing, but also a confessional. It is awesome for me to realize sometimes that none but the patient, God, and I knows about what we are discussing. It is even more awesome to realize that sometimes I am the voice of God to him. How essential then it is for me to do two things: first, to point out that I, too, am merely a man, and at best can only react to him and advise as I see things to be; second, to keep myself unspotted before a holy God so that He can use me as His instrument of healing. It is unavoidable that my personal theology will have some influence on my therapy. Certainly to be an atheist tends to affect the way a therapist will advise his patients. I must therefore be not only doctrinally sound but also pure in heart, to be usable by God. Paul Tournier, the contemporary Swiss Christian psychiatrist, starts every day in prayer for his patients. He says, "My nine o'clock session is with God."

I have prayed for the gift of healing. I am no faith healer, but I see it as my responsibility to my patients to stay constantly in close touch with the divine source of wisdom. He, the Holy Spirit, can then give me the thoughts and words which can help to bring comfort and healing to the needy who place their trust in me. As a Christian therapist I must truly have empathy. This is sometimes called "your pain in my heart." It consists of concern, warmth, genuine interest, and *agapē* love. The source of this quality of love is God Himself. I cannot love all my patients in my own strength. I have to ask God to give me love for them. Without compassion and caring, all my knowledge and experience is vain and empty. To the extent that God has seen fit to use me in this way, I believe I have been given the quality of love and the gift of healing for which I asked.

Christian psychotherapy is not magical. It is a blending of common sense, good professionally taught principles of psychological treatment, and the inspiration of the wisdom of the Holy Spirit. This is mediated through passages of Scripture or by the unexpected spontaneous development of an idea in the mind of either the patient or therapist, which is then elaborated and clarified by their shared dialogue. It is at the level of the spirit that true repentance and assurance of forgiveness meet. Healing of the mind and spirit combine to lead to change and growth toward normality. Inasmuch as Jesus was the only completely "normal" man who ever lived, growth towards normality is growth toward being like Him.

In the case of the nonbelieving patient, my responsibility is to relate to him primarily as a physician, without any evangelistic preaching, but nevertheless to let him know where I stand and what my beliefs are. I feel that it is ethical to tell a patient that I believe that there is a spiritual dimension, and therefore an additional source of help to him, through a relationship with God in Christ. If the patient is not responsive I do not pursue the issue. If he is, I will follow up his interest within the ethical boundaries of my professional obligation to him. It is gratifying over the years to look back at histories of patients who were initially ignorant of the potential changes which Christ could make in their lives. Many of them made some measure of progress towards a deeper understanding of their relationship to God. In a few cases they yielded to Christ as personal Saviour, either during treatment or sometime later.

Twenty-five million evangelical Protestants and also many devout Roman Catholic believers in the USA represent a significant subgroup in the potential therapeutic community. This subgroup is antagonistic to atheistic psychoanalysis and suspicious of newer therapeutic ideas or practices if they seem to threaten or challenge scriptural principles. These millions of people, however, will nevertheless have medical and psychiatric needs. Christian psychotherapy is primarily concerned with supplying these needs. It is, I believe, a healing ministry of a specialized form provided by God primarily for those of His people who are afflicted with all manner of diseases. The true church, the Body of Christ, is a spiritual fellowship which can be an additional corrective or healing resource to the troubled and suffering believer.

The key to success is the development under God of a relationship between doctor and patient based on their mutual desire to see God's will done in their lives. Mutual trust and respect between them can lead to *agapē* love and even some measure of controlled human affection. The skillful use of this affectional transference can be a therapeutic asset if it leads to a greater willingness on the part of the patient to be influenced by the therapist to make those changes which will bring him more closely to emotional health and in line with God's plan for his life. Ultimately Christ Himself should become the object of transference.

God speaks to man primarily through his mind, his emotions being secondarily involved. A man's appreciation of God's purposes for him must be understood with full rational conscious awareness if he is to react appropriately to guidance. Contamination with emotional influences arising within himself as a result of previous behavior patterns, anxiety, or selfish desires, will adversely affect the the obedient carrying out of what he knows with his mind to be right. Only unrepented sin can block communication between God and man. Both patient and therapist have this additional resource of divine wisdom. Many times in difficult moments with a patient I have uttered the emergency silent prayer, "Lord, what do I say now?" The answer usually comes by the patient providing a new line of discussion which leads to a fresh approach to the difficult subject. Sometimes a new idea seems to arise spontaneously in my own mind, the Holy Spirit connecting together the appropriate intracerebral neural pathways to produce the proper thoughts needed. The Holy Spirit seems to be able to put ideas into the receptive mind of the man or woman in touch with God. We know that a mature and experienced Christian steeped in a knowledge of the Scriptures seems more readily able to recognize, understand, and utilize thoughts which are consistent with its teachings. How vitally important, therefore, it is for the Christian therapist not only to know his Bible well but also to remain constantly refreshing his memory of God's Word by regular daily, prayerful Bible study.

Christian psychotherapy, however, is much more than the use of Bible verses and prayer. It is based on the whole message of God's revelation to man and the philosophical principles of the Gospel of man's redemption in Christ. Preeminent among these principles is the doctrine of the sovereignty of God. God rules and chastens. God knows and purposes. God loves and forgives.

Nothing happens in the daily life of the believer outside of God's executive or permissive will. Even our deliberate sin is included in the "all things" that "work together for good to them that love God" and who are "called according to his purpose" (*see* Romans 8:28). There is either a temporal or an eternal purpose in human suffering. If it is temporal, it is usually a chastening-for-righteousness experience (*see* Hebrews 12:11) and we will be given the understanding of it in our time. If it is an eternal purpose, we will understand it in eternity. Whichever it is, Christians are given by God the strength to bear the suffering and to accept that which cannot in this life be changed. God also, however, does bestow some measure of healing skills to man to help those thus in need. Hence Christian psychotherapy—a new developing treatment modality given by God to this generation to meet the needs of His children in these preapocalyptic times.

One of the most valuable resources available in Christian psychotherapy is the integrated balance of faith and hope. Faith and trust in God, combined with faith and trust in the doctor, once established in the patient, is a major first step in the direction of healing. Hope is next, and here the therapist has the responsibility to inspire his patient. The power of suggestion, rightly used, can help to develop in the depressed or anxious sufferer, thoughts and feelings of good expectations, confidence in the future, and belief in himself and in all who care for him. These will lead to a powerful motivation to think positively and work towards realistic objectives which will represent changes within himself, in his life-style, and in those of his relationships which he either needs or desires. Anxiety and depression, in and of themselves, are not to be seen as sinful. They are normal human responses to common stresses or stimuli.

Another principle of the Scriptures is the righteousness of God. Unredeemed sinful man cannot have communion with a holy God. Justified, redeemed sinners have that communion through their personal acceptance of Christ's atonement. However, though we can never lose our salvation, we can lose communion with God in this world, and much of our rewards in heaven. Though not all mental or emotional suffering can be explained by this loss of communion, much of it can be. For the Christian continuing to live in a state of unconfessed and unrepented sin, spiritual separation from God is the inevitable result. This in turn can lead to a wide variety of carnal actions which often result in unhappiness, dissatisfaction, frustration, guilt, resentment, bitterness, hostility, jealousy, or such neurotic symptoms as anxiety and depression. Unlike secular treatment, Christian psychotherapy has to concern itself with the issues of right and wrong. We believe that absolute standards are clearly taught in the

Word of God and no amount of rationalizing can effect escape from the results of transgression. The Christian therapist does not teach his patient to accept his failures and adapt himself to the consequences of human weakness. The counselor has the responsibility to point out the areas in which sin in the life of the sufferer has led to his neurotic symptoms or unhappy life situations. Education and teaching of moral and scriptural principles are an important part of the healing process. A biblical value system is a solid foundation for both spiritual and psychological healing. If the patient claims to be a Christian believer, such basic sins as selfishness, pride, and greed (which can lead to other sins) have to be clearly revealed to him and urgent exhortation to eliminate or control them must be made. Once he can be lead to the point of being willing to repent, the power of the Holy Spirit, the greatest power in all of the created universe, is instantly available to him to remove his self-destructive desires and actions.

This leads to another principle which is implicit rather than explicit in the Old and New Testaments. This is the fact that God has given to all men the ability to make free choices or decisions. In a sense, God has temporarily and partially reduced His control of man to the extent that He permits the exercise of free will and its resultant courses of action. In the hereafter, God will reclaim absolute control of all His Creation, but for now He has chosen to bring into existence creatures which He desires to love Him and serve Him voluntarily. With this gift of free will, however, God has also given man both the knowledge of right and wrong and a sense of responsibility to use it appropriately. It is man's irresponsible and selfish use of free will in choosing contrary to God's best plan for him that has led to all the disaster and misery throughout human history. Therefore, a vital principle of healing is the restoration of a sense of responsibility in the sufferer to lead him back to the point where he will decide once more to allow his life's direction to be conformed to that of God's plan. Involved in this is a willingness, in humility, to forgive the wrongs done to him by others; in all things, even disappointments, to give thanks; and to believe by faith that God has a definite purpose for his life.

This responsibility is not confined to spiritual decisions. Patients must be held responsible for all the consequences of their thoughts, feelings, and actions. Even though the symptoms of anxiety and depression may prove to be of at least partial biochemical origin, the ways in which patients react to these symptoms are within their responsibility to control. Some people can apparently tolerate physical pain more easily than others, but I do not believe that their nervous systems are any less sensitive. My ability to continue to function responsibly in spite of physical or emotional pain is achieved by my desire to do what I ought. This is not stoicism. It is Christian discipline and self-control. "If any man will come after me, let him deny himself, and take up his cross, and follow me" (*see* Matthew 16:24).

To the extent that neurotic symptoms are of chemical origin, temporary use of antidepressants and tranquilizers can be of expedience. I only prescribe such medications for crisis-intervention situations or as an adjunct to short-term therapy. With continuing psychotherapy, the majority of successful treatment outcomes reflect the patient's ability to feel and function well without their help.

A final factor that needs to be borne in mind by therapists is the observable evidence that people are different. Even though a headache or anxiety may be of equal pain in one man as in his neighbor, the fact is that *one* is better able to tolerate it. Both have an equal responsibility to control their reactions to symptoms, and this responsibility must be impressed upon all patients regardless of their strengths or weaknesses. The fact remains that some people are inferior to others in their ability to handle and cope with pressures. Some are basically healthy, with good ego-strength, optimistic self-confidence and the ability to triumph over difficulties. Others with low self-esteem wallow in self-pity and become chronically dependent on the strength and help of others. Traditionally, Christians have always helped the downtrodden and those who are going through times of adversity. The Christian psychotherapist, however, has to be very careful to distinguish between those who are sick or inferior through no fault of their own, and those who have adopted a life-style which demands and expects to be taken care of by others. For the former, we are called to be Good Samaritans and give all the support and help we can. For the latter, the malingerers, we should exercise Spirit-inspired directive leadership to point them back in the direction of responsible living.

The development of Bible-based Christian psychotherapy is one of the most exciting pioneering ventures for the years ahead. These principles of healing merely superficially outline some of the ideas which Christian therapists like myself will be evaluating and developing in the immediate future. The chapters which follow enlarge on some of the thoughts contained herein, especially as they apply to man's development and experience from birth to death.

2

....

MIND, EMOTIONS, AND WILL
IN THE CHRISTIAN EXPERIENCE

Christianity is not just a religion. It is a way of life, and for the believer it is more than an intellectual assent to a list of doctrines. It is preeminently a relationship: an individual personal relationship between the believer and his Saviour and Lord, between the true Christian and Jesus Christ. This chapter deals with the thoughts, feelings, and decisions related to the acquisition of this relationship and its psychological and emotional components. The rest of the book deals with some of the ways, good and bad, in which the Christian's experience affects him throughout life.

In eternity past, God decided to create beings capable of loving Him voluntarily. The most profound theologian cannot answer the question of why God did this. The fact is that it happened. On a human level one can only compare it with the joy of having children. As my son and daughter grow and begin to reflect back to me the love that I have for them, it is an experience of the deepest emotional pleasure and satisfaction.

For us to love God voluntarily we had to have free will, and with this gift came the unavoidable possibility that it could be used to hate or ignore God rather than to love Him. Whatever may be your beliefs about evolution or special Creation, the important fact is that at a moment in the prehistoric past, God began to communicate with man. I personally believe the Adam-and-Eve story and accept it as the explanation for the origin of sin. If you believe that evolutionary theory accounts for the ascent of man you will agree that there came a time when man's brain had developed to the point

at which he became capable of rational thought, a conscious awareness, and an ability to make choices. However we view it, human
history records the inescapable fact that man is capable of doing
both good and evil, of using his free will to make decisions affecting
himself and others for better or worse.

The will is affected by two influences: thoughts and emotions,
both of which are manifestations of basic needs. Thoughts are pro-
ductions of the conscious mind which is anatomically located in
the cerebral cortex, the most highly developed, and evolutionarily
the newest, part of the brain. Emotions have not been so definitely
localized. The hypothalamus in the primitive brainstem seems to
be an area extensively activated in their production, but much of
the rest of the central nervous system may also be involved. In
terms of evolution, anthropologists tell us that it was when the
cerebral cortex had developed a mind that was able to control the
emotions that true man, Homo sapiens, came into existence. Prior
to this time, primitive hominids were not capable of anything but
the crudest forms of communication and social structure. The significance of Adam and Eve is that, with their creation, God finally
produced fully developed human beings whose minds were capable
of communication not only with each other but with Himself.

In Genesis 4:2 we read, "And Abel was a keeper of sheep, but
Cain was a tiller of the ground." This would seem to be a good
description of the primitive agriculture and domestication of animals
of Neolithic man who lived about 10,000 years ago. However, Professor James Buswell, a Christian anthropologist who has written
several articles on the antiquity of Adam in the *Journal of the
American Scientific Affiliation,* believes that the Garden of Eden
existed much earlier than that time. According to Genesis 2, the
Garden was located in what is now the Middle East and north-
eastern Africa, south as far as Ethiopia. Verse 15 states, "And the
Lord God took the man, and put him into the garden of Eden to
dress it and to keep it." In the original statement of man's creation,
God said, "And let them have dominion over the fish of the sea,
fowl, cattle, and every creeping thing" (*see* Genesis 1:26). Latest
archeological findings indicate that as far back as the lower (earlier)

Paleolithic period (20–50,000 years ago) men hunted game, collected plant food, and wandered around in single-family groups, larger settled habitations coming slightly later.

The Bible is not a scientific textbook, however, and exact dates are not important. We do not know how long Adam and Eve were in the Garden before they disobeyed God and were cast out. Since they were not subject to pathological degenerative processes, it could have been the thousands of years between the old and new Stone Ages. (It is assumed that the 930 years of Adam's life [*see* Genesis 5:5] were counted from the date he was expelled from Eden, since before that date he was immortal.) The time eventually came, however, when they allowed their emotions to have a greater influence than their minds upon their wills.

Primitive urges momentarily superseded rational conscience and they chose to eat the forbidden fruit. It is the same today with us— their descendants. When the instinctual drives of the *id* dominate the sensible controls of the *superego* (when emotions dominate mind) the will or decision-making component of the *ego* is likely to choose that which is wrong.

The doctrine of Original Sin is an observable fact of human experience. The Prophet Jeremiah wrote, "The heart is deceitful above all things, and desperately wicked: who can know it?" (Jeremiah 17:9). We cannot blame God by claiming it is all His fault since He made us the way we are. We still make our choices with our free wills and we are held responsible. The philosophy of determinism states that all our actions and moral choices are the results of previous influences, and that we are not responsible for them. This is diametrically opposed to the clear message of Scripture both with regard to the doctrine of free will and in view of the teaching that God is a righteous judge who holds men accountable for their actions.

Now God is a *Holy* God into whose presence nothing defiled can enter. After the rejection from Eden, therefore, there was nothing which sinful man could do to effect a restoration of fellowship with Him. God Himself had to redeem His lost creation, that is, to buy it back. He is in the process of achieving this in three stages. The first was His revelation of Himself to man through the history of the chosen people of Israel and the writings of Moses and the prophets. The third stage will be the final consummation of all redeemed mankind when, after the Last Judgment, we will enter into His presence to serve Him without sin for all the eternal ages. We are presently living in the second stage, or the Age of Grace, in which God gives to every man the opportunity to become individually reconciled with Him. It is the process related to this stage, and man's psychological and emotional involvement in it, which is the subject of the rest of this chapter.

God's plan of redemption was infinitely costly since nothing short of perfection could effect reconciliation between defiled mankind and the awesome blinding purity of the Almighty Being. Indeed, only God Himself could achieve it and He had to come in person, in human form, to do it. "God was in Christ, reconciling the world unto himself" (*see* 2 Corinthians 5:19). We do not know why God chose this method but He agreed to accept the shed blood of Christ on the cross as full payment for the sins of all mankind. Paul wrote to the Roman believers: "But God commendeth his love toward us, in that, while we were yet sinners, Christ died for us. Much more then, being now justified by his blood, we shall be saved from wrath through him" (Romans 5:8, 9). Earlier he had written: "For all have sinned, and come short of the glory of God; Being justified freely by his grace through the redemption that is in Christ Jesus: Therefore we conclude that a man is justified by faith without the deeds of the law" (Romans 3:23, 24, 28).

By faith—this is the key, not only to becoming a Christian but also to continuing to be a Christian. It is in the exercise of faith that man's mind, will, and emotions are involved. "And what is faith? Faith gives substance to our hopes, and makes us certain of realities we do not see" (Hebrews 11:1 NEB). Faith is *not* believing in something that is untrue or even in something for which there is no evidence. It is believing in something for which there is no proof. If there *were* proof we would be compelled to believe by the sheer argument of logic. The force of gravity is a proven scientific fact. Not to believe in it could end in disaster. It is a matter of logic, not faith. That God raised Christ from the dead cannot be proven, but can be believed through faith because of the great weight of evidence supporting its historicity. (Sincere open-minded sceptics are urged to read *Who Moved the Stone?* by Frank Morison. It is written by a lawyer who set out to prove that the Resurrection of Christ did not take place, but who became so convinced by the very evidence he was investigating that he was converted.)

To take the initial step of faith requires all three parts of the human personality: the mind, the will, and the emotions. The *mind* has first to examine the evidence and thereby become intellectually convinced that the basic principles of God's revelation to man in the Scriptures and in the person of Christ are truth. The *will* has to make the decision to appropriate this body of truth into itself and thereby accept Christ as Saviour and Lord in the person's life. Finally, the *emotions* are involved in sealing the contract by making a personal commitment to discipleship. Faith is a gift from God offered to all men, but it requires an individual response by the whole personality before it can be effective unto salvation. It has to be solidly focused on the historic facts of the Incarnation and Resurrection of Christ. If feelings are allowed to rear their ugly heads, assurance of salvation can be jeopardized. This is why people suffering from anxiety or depression frequently feel they have lost their faith and therefore their eternal security. In reality our security lies in the facts of history, not in our variable feelings. When faith has been exercised by all three parts of the personality, God enters as He promised. God Himself becomes my personal heavenly Father, Christ my personal Saviour and Lord, and the Holy Spirit my personal Guide and Comforter. I am given assurance of forgiveness, security of eternal salvation, and power to live the Christian life.

This is but the beginning of the Christian experience, sometimes described as being born again as a new creation in Christ, or being converted from a life of selfishness and sin to a life yielded to God's control and guidance. We now have to go on to the process of growth: development from being a babe in Christ to the attainment of Christian maturity. It costs nothing to *become* a Christian. It costs everything to *be* a Christian. It costs an absolute surrender of the self to God's continuing revelation of His will for our lives on a day-by-day basis. The worldly Christian who makes only a partial surrender will be continually miserable because of the internal conflict of interests pulling in opposite directions. ". . . . Ye cannot serve God and mammon" (Matthew 6:24).

The World, the Flesh, and the Devil

It is said that a picture is worth a thousand words. To save words and time, keep a finger in page 37 to observe a diagram which summarizes the next few pages. It is a useful, descriptive model to facilitate the understanding of several scriptural principles.

The *superego* or conscience is that part of man's personality which acts as a control on his thoughts and behavior. In human terms it represents the end product of all the influences of parents, teachers, and culture which work to conform an individual to the expectations and behavioral norms of his particular social environment. In the Christian, the superego absorbs the additional molding influences of the principles of Scripture and the obligation to do God's will as mediated to him through the power of the Holy Spirit. The superego in turn influences the *ego* or real self through the mind and emotions.

There are, of course, many conflicting influences, and it is the responsibility of the ego, through the gift of free will, to evaluate, balance, and choose between the different pros and cons of all necessary decisions. These decisions lead to actions, and repeated patterns of actions can lead to the development of habits. These in turn affect the character structure of the individual, which ultimately affects his eternal destiny. For example, a man who allows the Holy Spirit to influence his superego, mind, and emotions will make a decision for Christ. He will then find that his life-style thereafter leads through a process of sanctification to the development of Christ-centered actions and habits. These will eventually

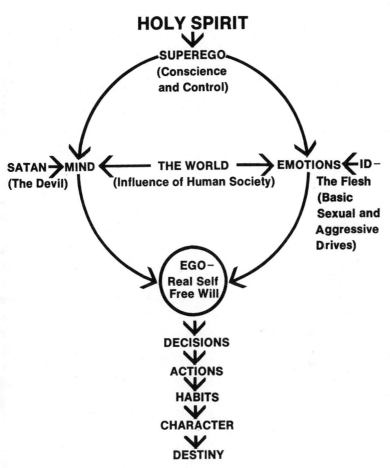

manifest a godly character destined for everlasting life serving his Lord.

The Christian pilgrim has to cope with three contrary influences tending to direct him off his course—the world, the flesh, and the devil.

The world, as used in the New Testament, describes our human society, essentially organized on selfish principles. It is *not* the planet Earth, God's Creation. This is a thing of beauty and grandeur. Nor is it the individual men and women whom God created and for whose sins Christ died. It *is* the system of thoughts and conduct, the unworthy motives, the warped standards and inverted sense of values which have pervaded our civilization. Our Western society and all other cultures are inherently hostile to the God revealed in the Bible and tend to delude men into thinking that they do not need Him. Living under this world system, the individual's mind, emotions, and will are all influenced by its ubiquitous presence. For the practicing Christian this will mean that he may experience misunderstanding, ridicule, rejection, and even martyrdom.

Jesus said, ". . . because ye are not of the world, but I have chosen you out of the world, therefore the world hateth you" (John 15:19). Half a century later, the apostle who recorded those words added: "Love not the world, neither the things that are in the world . . . (1 John 2:15).

The flesh, from the Greek word *sarx* in the New Testament, is usually used to describe the influence of those human passions which are contrary to the influence of the Spirit in man. Freud described human sexual and aggressive drives as the *id.* These drives are healthy and necessary for living a satisfying and fulfilling life. They are manifested through the emotions which influence the ego whose responsibility is to balance their effect with the controlling input of the superego. When the influence of the id or flesh dominates, then the will is likely to make a sinful or selfish choice.

The works of the flesh are listed by Paul in Galatians 5:19–21. Here are described man's immorality, selfishness, perversions, pride, and greed. They are not confined to pagans, however. The born-again Christian must be wary since he has two natures, the old and the new. The old nature or flesh "lusteth against the Spirit, and the Spirit against the flesh: and these are contrary the one to the other: so that ye cannot do the things that ye would" (Galatians 5:17). Vividly describing this internal conflict, Paul writes: "For the good that I would I do not: but the evil which I would not, that I do. For I delight in the law of God after the inward man: But I see another law in my members, warring against the law of my mind

. . . . So then with the mind I myself serve the law of God; but with the flesh the law of sin" (Romans 7:19, 22, 23, 25).

The new nature has the potential for victory: "For the law of the Spirit of life in Christ Jesus hath made me free from the law of sin and death" (Romans 8:2). This Spirit, via the superego, influences the mind and the ego to control the flesh and emotions so that the will can make a balanced and appropriate decision.

The devil—Satan influences the mind or intellect and causes us to doubt God. "And he said unto the woman, Yea, hath God said? [Then] ye shall not surely die" (*see* Genesis 3:1, 4). He makes us want to resist God's controlling intervention and tempts Christians to become independent of God—to act to negate the labors of others working for God's Kingdom. He tempts us to rely on our own strength and to "do our own thing." He tries to destroy our faith when things go wrong by making us doubt the truth of Scripture and the assurance of salvation. We resist his lies by standing on God's Word and its promises.

Other fallen angels are invisible evil spirits or demons deployed on earth under Satan's directive control. "For we wrestle not against flesh and blood, but against principalities, against powers, against the rulers of the darkness of this world, against spiritual wickedness in high places" (Ephesians 6:12). This verse makes the point that Satan's main strategy is to work through the minds of people in positions of leadership and influence—politicians, teachers, doctors, lawyers, and preachers. Evil spirits also undermine the Kingdom of God on earth by either direct resistance or, more subtly, through the dissemination of false religious doctrine—making Christians too lukewarm and lacking in zeal or destroying their brotherly fellowship by causing them to dispute with each other. As with Eve, the Evil One, through his subordinates beguiles us to seek a "superior" religious experience and tempts us away from a simple faith in Christ.

Spiritual Growth

The process of spiritual growth in the Christian experience involves essentially the nurturing of an ever-deepening relationship with Christ. This relationship at once gives the believer inner security, a sense of identity, and fellowship. He not only has the security of forgiveness and salvation, he also knows that God loves, protects, guides, and provides. This security gives a sense of tranquility, uplift, and inner peace which can calm anxiety and fear and elevate depressive moods. The sense of identity the Christian acquires gives him confidence to go about his work boldly and with a thrilling sense of purpose. As a child of God he knows that he is fulfilling a part of God's eternal plan and that he is important as a vital member of a team. He is also blessed by the joy of fellowship and communion with other believers. New friendships are made and, in joining a church, he receives a source of continuing instruction in the Word of God and inspiration and encouragement to continue his spiritual pilgrimage.

All of these blessings, however, are but the icing on the cake. The real core of the Christian experience is the joy of the indwelling Christ. In His Upper Room exhortation to the eleven remaining disciples after the Last Supper, Jesus said: "Abide in me, and I in you. As the branch cannot bear fruit of itself, except it abide in the vine; no more can ye, except ye abide in me. I am the vine, ye are the branches: He that abideth in me, and I in him, the same bringeth forth much fruit: for without me ye can do nothing" (John 15:4, 5).

Abiding means to have no unrepented sin separating the believer from his Lord and no interest or activity into which he cannot take his Lord with him. Abiding also involves taking all worries and burdens to Christ and drawing from Him wisdom, strength, guidance, peace, joy, love, and power over temptation and sin. Abiding does not imply a continuing conscious awareness of Christ, but it does imply such a closeness that this awareness can be activated at any time for some service which the Lord requires.

Abiding involves prayer, meditation, study of the Scriptures, and worshipful adoration not only on a disciplined, daily basis but also at any other appropriate time as the Lord leads. All of this involves the use of the mind, emotions, and will. I communicate with God in the act of prayerful study of the Bible and by the Holy Spirit speaking directly to my mind. Two-way communication with God is an intense intellectual exercise. It is the highest activity of the brain and sometimes the most difficult. Prayer is essentially thinking, talking to God, and listening to Him by turning verses of Scripture into inspired means of influence on both mind and emotions.

It is essential to the Christian experience that prayer not be used merely as a means of supplication. "Ask, and it shall be given you; seek, and ye shall find; knock, and it shall be opened unto you" (Matthew 7:7). God is more concerned with supplying us all our needs than we are ourselves. We need only to tell Him once and trust Him to provide. Prayer time spent repeatedly craving something is selfish and wasteful. "But seek ye first the kingdom of God, and his righteousness; and all these things shall be added unto you" (Matthew 6:33).

Intercession for others, thanksgiving for all God's blessings, and adoring praise of Christ for who He is and what He has done should occupy the bulk of our spiritual efforts in prayer.

Finally, the key to success in the Christian experience is the believer's responsibility to find out God's will for him, to become willing to do it, and then to go forth and obediently carry out what he knows to be right. Prayer in this regard is preeminently the means which God uses to bring the Christian's will into conformity with His will. Remember that the Holy Spirit primarily influences the mind or intellect. If this influence dominates the emotions and brings them into conformity as well, there will be no conflict. Prayer is a means whereby the mind wins over the emotions so that the Christian will not only *know* what is right but *will have the desire to do it*. The mind and emotions then present a united front to the will, which thereupon makes the decisions and motivates the believer to action. His obedience is then rewarded with joy and peace and the satisfaction of knowing that he is in the center of God's will for his life.

This all sounds like an unattainable ideal, perfection this side of heaven. The chapters that follow deal with some of the hard realities of the Christian life and the failures and difficulties that accompany it. Hopefully, some answers, both psychological and spiritual, will also be found which will help the pilgrim on his exciting and challenging road upwards to the celestial Kingdom.

3

··

PSYCHOLOGICAL DEFENSE
MECHANISMS

When a person becomes a Christian he does not cease to be a normal human personality. His mental and emotional makeup, his character structure, his temperamental type, and his patterns of behavior still remain basically the same. He is different, however, in that he has yielded himself to the influence of the Holy Spirit, who, through the long and sometimes painful experience of sanctification, can effect very basic changes in the mind and heart of the willing believer. This process of growing in grace can take a lifetime, and even on their deathbeds few saints would claim to have reached a condition of absolute surrender of their wills to God. Most Christians still allow habits of thought and action developed over earlier years to control their reactions to various circumstances.

It is normal to attempt to defend oneself for the sake of self-preservation. Physical or verbal evasive action can be seen all around us every day at home or at work. Not telling the full truth is a typical example. Not so obvious are the unseen defense mechanisms continuously at work in our minds—striving to prevent or reduce emotional pain. These processes are not necessarily dishonest or sinful, indeed some may be needful or even occasionally healthy. They help to satisfy needs for affection, security, self-esteem, and inner peace.

Their use in the Christian experience is complicated by the fact that the believer has the obligation, and hopefully the desire, to be honest before God in all his thinking. He also is vulnerable to experiencing unnecessary or exaggerated guilt as a result of his less compromising **superego** or conscience. This part of his personality represents a system of values learned from parents, society, or his religion and tends to control basic instinctual drives operating on the *pleasure principle*, collectively described as the *id*. The *ego* or real self caught in the conflict between these extremes operates on the *reality principle* because it deals with the hard facts of the external environment. To reduce the pain of this conflict the ego's primary defense is repression, which is basic to all other defense mechanisms.

Repression is the involuntary exclusion from conscious awareness of painful or conflicting thoughts, impulses, or memories which are pushed down into the unconscious. Although they usually remain dormant they can be resurrected by thinking in response to specific probing questions, by remembered associations, and in dreams. Forgetting is a form of repression, a defense against cluttering up our minds with memories of unnecessary details of bygone years. Repression has the effect of reducing anxiety and avoiding reality. Memories associated with guilt, shame, or lowered self-esteem are especially likely to be repressed.

Herein is the special problem for the Christian. In order for him to be in uninterrupted fellowship with God it is essential for all past sins to be confessed and repented. When the Christian accepts the shed blood of Christ as full atonement for his sins, this covers *all* sins—past, present, and future—whether remembered or not, and whether committed deliberately or in ignorance. Therefore, his eternal justification is not at stake, but his spiritual growth in this life *is*. The problem is that repressed impulses retain some measure of influence on behavior traits, patterns of thinking, and styles of emotional reactions. If any of these tend to cause the Christian to speak or act contrary to his understanding of God's will for his life, he will suffer from internal conflict. This conflict might reach the point where it is necessary for the repressed material to be brought to consciousness and thence removed by rational understanding. This can often be achieved by pastoral counseling in depth or analytic psychotherapy. Many Christians, however, have testified that their own disciplined Bible study and importunate prayers have achieved the same unburdening results. It seems that the Holy Spirit has brought back memories of the unpleasant experiences which originally caused the feelings of guilt and low self-esteem. Honest facing up to past failures and sins, with assurance of divine forgiveness, has led to removal of the weights and a refreshing freedom to start again with a clean slate.

Not all repressed material needs to be exposed. Much of it is harmless, but the sincere Christian knows that God will reveal all that he needs to understand to enable him to remove all hindrances to his spiritual growth. Honest admission and repentance of past failures leads to restoration of fellowship and renewed progress in the right direction.

Suppression is the conscious analogue of repression. It is the intentional and deliberate exclusion of undesirable thoughts from conscious awareness. It is not an unconscious mechanism, but a positive act on the part of the mind to control or remove unacceptable thinking traits. If my mind wanders onto some pleasurable fantasy when I am trying to study the Bible or a professional journal, I abruptly discipline my thoughts and force them back into line with the job at hand. If the fantasy returns and persists I outmaneuver it by replacing it with another pleasurable fantasy over which I have more control. My personal favorite is to imagine myself playing on the golf course near my home. After my three-hundred-yard drive, perfect approach shot, and birdie putt have all been indulged in, I have long since forgotten the original distraction and can get back to the book again.

Frequently Christian patients come to my office in great distress because of "evil thoughts." These, on further questioning, usually turn out to be sexual or blasphemous thought-patterns which are destroying their inner peace. My responsibility is to help them to understand the cause of the obsessive thoughts by investigating with them some possible origins and early experiences which led to their development.

Obsessive thinking is a neurotic trait which is a manifestation of hidden anxiety. It occurs most frequently in individuals who are excessively concerned with conformity and adherence to high moral or religious standards. Christians, for example, raised in very rigid, overinhibited, fundamentalist homes tend to develop unrealistically high goals for themselves which are beyond the limits of their reasonable abilities. They become overconscientious, overdutiful and self-condemnatory, suffer from false guilt, and are totally incapable of relaxing. I try to help them understand their backgrounds and encourage them to practice suppression of their disturbing thoughts by replacing them with more easily controllable substitutes. As soon as the unwanted thoughts or memories come into their minds they train themselves to substitute more wholesome ones. Practice makes perfect in this venture and I usually find that suppression is eventually successful. Unless it is used to avoid some responsibility, it is most often healthy, and not sinful. For the Christian, no challenge to disciplined and wholesome thinking is better expressed than Paul's exhortation to the Philippians: "Finally, brethren, whatsoever things are true, honest, just, pure, lovely, of good report; if there be any virtue, and if there be any praise, think on these things" (*see* Philippians 4:8).

The *Unpardonable Sin* is a special kind of obsessional thought-pattern which I frequently encounter in my psychiatric practice. This is a problem in people who are believers, but are afraid that they have committed the Unpardonable Sin. Without exception in my experience, they have been unquestionably born again, and testify that they were once sure they were saved, but now have doubts. I have never heard a pagan express this fear. Invariably these Christians also describe other symptoms which indicate to me that their real problems are not, in fact, spiritual, but psychological or emotional. The following conditions can cause a Christian to believe erroneously that he has unpardonably sinned or in some way lost his salvation: paranoia, acute anxiety, endogenous depression, and some forms of schizophrenia.

At the level of his ability to understand, I explain that his eternal security is based not on his feelings or confused thinking but on the historic facts of the Incarnation and Resurrection of Jesus Christ.

He is eternally saved because at some moment in past time he appropriated for himself the shed blood of Christ as full atonement for his sins. Christ is now his Saviour and Lord and this relationship is sealed and unbreakable for all the ages.

In the twelfth chapter of Matthew, the Lord healed a blind and dumb man possessed with a devil. The Pharisees, when they heard about it, said He had done it "by Beelzebub, the prince of the devils" (*see* vs. 22–24). *They therefore ascribed to the devil the work of the Spirit of God.* This, and only this, according to the entire Bible, is the one sin that cannot be pardoned. Jesus states this to them explicitly in His reply: ". . . All manner of sin and blasphemy shall be forgiven unto men: but the blasphemy against the Holy Ghost shall not be forgiven unto men. And whosoever speaketh against the Son of Man, it shall be forgiven him: but whosoever speaketh against the Holy Ghost, it shall not be forgiven him, neither in this world, neither in the world to come" (Matthew 12:31, 32 and *see* Mark 3:29 and Luke 12:10).

The great contemporary Hebrew-Christian scholar, Dr. Henry J. Heydt, formerly of Beth Sar Shalom in New York City and now retired in Florida, states:

> The reason it is unpardonable is because the conviction of sin is the work of the Holy Spirit, and when He is thus blasphemed He completely withdraws, and conviction cannot possibly take place. *It follows that a person in this condition has no concern whatever about sin or his eternal state. It also follows that no person who is born of the Spirit could commit this sin.* It need hardly be said that such a sin is knowingly and deliberately committed, or it would not come under the category of blasphemy. [*Italics* are added.]

If, therefore, someone does have a concern that he might have committed this sin, he could not, in fact, have done so. Removal of the Spirit causes such a blasphemer to care no more. He goes to a lost eternity with no concern or anxiety. If a person *does* have anxiety or a feeling of guilt, this means that the Spirit is *still* working on his heart and mind, has therefore *not* left him, and he therefore can still be saved. His anxiety and guilt are the result of other sins, *not* the Unpardonable Sin.

There are two well-known passages in Hebrews which have a bearing on this subject. We read: "For it is impossible for those who were once enlightened . . . If they shall fall away, to renew them again unto repentance . . ." (Hebrews 6:4–6). Likewise in a later passage: "For if we sin wilfully after that we have received the knowledge of the truth, there remaineth no more sacrifice for sins . . ." (Hebrews 10:26). With regard to these passages, Dr. Heydt makes the point that the people referred to were not fully committed believers, but merely those who professed to be interested, even up to the point of repentance, but were not truly saved. The truly saved person is eternally secure:

. . . He that heareth my word, and believeth on him that sent me, hath everlasting life, and shall not come into condemnation; but is passed from death unto life.

John 5:24

My sheep hear my voice, and I know them, and they follow me: And I give unto them eternal life; and they shall never perish, neither shall any man pluck them out of my hand.

John 10:27, 28

Rationalization is deluding oneself by giving a socially acceptable and apparently logical explanation for an act or decision which was motivated by unconscious repressed impulses. This is not the same as lying, which is a deliberate, consciously produced falsehood for the purpose of misleading another. Rationalization is an unconsciously produced falsehood for the purpose of defending against the pain of guilt or shame. In fact, human nature is such that self-centered and instinctive influences on decisions are much stronger than ethical ones. Ethical principles and the knowledge of right and wrong are mediated by the superego and dominate the conscious mind. In their ability to control behavior they are no match for the basic drives of the id which dominate the unconscious mind—hence the internal conflict that the ego has to arbitrate. Usually, rationalizations do contain at least some element of truth which the ego then unduly emphasizes to conceal the real motive for the action in question. Behavior is influenced by a complicated mixture of many good and bad motives. By the process of rationalization we carefully select only the acceptable ones and convince ourselves that this is the full truth.

The Christian has a powerful resource to deal with this problem once he has come to the point of being willing to acknowledge truth. "I am the way, the truth, and the life," said the Lord (*see* John 14:6). Jesus is truth. A personal relationship with Him, therefore, will reveal truth to the humble seeker. If I can become willing to admit and make restitution for unpleasant facts about my past, the Holy Spirit will show me the truth. *Retrospective falsification* is the term used to describe unconscious distortions of past experiences to conform to present emotional needs. These distortions need to be brought to conscious awareness. I must then exclude all attempts on my part at evasion, equivocation, or mental reservations of any kind. If I can do this I am given by God not only knowledge, but spiritual power to do what He has shown me to be right. This is tough to achieve because my stubborn will is so unyielding; but when, through prayerful repentance, I come to this point of surrender, the truth of God then takes over in my mind and heart and enables me to live the transparently honest and upright life which God requires. I will then no longer be living a lie and I will no longer need the protection of rationalization.

Identification is the unconscious modeling of oneself upon another. We often identify ourselves consciously with a cause, a political party, a set of values, attitudes of a group, or a religious system. We are usually consciously aware of these because they become part of our conversation and life-style. Identification with a person, however, is usually much more subtle and less obvious to consciousness. The most frequently observed example is a special form of identification known as *introjection* in which the developing child assimilates into his own superego many of the values, preferences, and attitudes of his parents and teachers. Since he later does the same with teen-aged peers, it is vital that positive parental and other adult influences be well established early, to provide him with standards to live by during these potentially rebellious years.

On the other hand, immoral, unloving, or criminal parents can produce children of the same ilk because their superegos have been misdirected before they were mature enough to have personal discernment. This is known as *hostile identification.*

Identification occurs frequently among adolescents and young adults. These young people are very easily influenced by those older than themselves, whom they respect. Hero worship, behavior conforming to leaders in their peer group, and emulation of admired elders are frequently encountered at both conscious and unconscious levels. Whether this mental mechanism is good or bad depends on the quality of the influence and the changeability of the recipient.

Christian faith is spread from believer to convert much more effectively on the one-to-one level than by preaching or discussions of doctrine. When I was a freshman at Cambridge, I was very impressed with a rugby-football player in my college who had many admirable qualities. I found myself identifying with many of his interests and desiring to have what he had, that I seemed to lack. This man was a strong Christian, but practiced a soft sell. Had he been more aggressive in propagating his views I am sure I would have rejected them—and him. As it was, my identification with him expanded to interest in his personal faith in Christ. My personal admiration for my friend was profoundly influential in helping me to make an eventual life-changing decision for Christ.

The ultimate in identification is that of the believer with Christ. Paul wrote to the Philippians, "Let this mind be in you, which was also in Christ Jesus" (Philippians 2:5). Growth in the Christian life consists largely of an ever-deepening identification by the disciple with his divine Master. The more Jesus becomes the One to whom I look, the more will I grow to be like Him and be usable by Him to influence others. Let us be "looking unto Jesus the author and finisher of our faith" (*see* Hebrews 12:2).

Projection is a defensive mechanism attributing undesirable or unacceptable thoughts or impulses to another person. A coed who was a member of a church young-adults group accused a fellow male member of making a pass at her. No such occurrence had actually taken place. In counseling it came out that the coed was sexually attracted to the boy, was jealous of his girl friend, and projected her denied sexual feelings onto him by her accusations. In the same church, two deacons had strongly opposing views about a decision that the board had to make. One of them had feelings of dislike and hostility toward the other, which he could not express in the church environment. He embarrassed the board by complaining untruthfully that the other man did not like him, thus projecting his own unacceptable feelings onto the other.

Projection is always bad because it invariably involves denying the truth. If allowed to grow to a serious pathological degree it can develop into paranoid delusions of persecution. In the psychotic these in turn could lead to auditory hallucinations in which the person hears voices accusing him, and these could result in violent defensive reactions against innocent people.

Denial is a failure to recognize and admit to obvious facts, implications, or consequences of thoughts, actions, or situations. A soldier, told by his sergeant that most men in the section would be killed or wounded in a forthcoming battle, said to himself, "I'm sure going to miss my comrades." People living close to the San Andreas fault deny the possibility that their homes may be damaged or destroyed in the next expected earthquake. An intelligent teen-age girl admitted she was having premarital sex with her boyfriend. Since neither was using any contraceptive method, they were totally denying the possibility of pregnancy. "It can't happen to me," is the basic unconscious thought-pattern involved in all of these situations. Consciously intolerable thoughts are disowned by unconscious rejection and protective nonawareness.

In the New Testament, denial is usually used to describe a *conscious* decision. "But whosoever shall deny me before men, him will I also deny before my Father which is in heaven" (Matthew 10:33). Peter's predicted denial of Christ was motivated by fear. His lies were a defense against the probable consequences of being identified with the prisoner before Pilate.

There are two references which seem to imply *unconscious denial*.

In his short letter to Titus, Paul, speaking of unbelievers, says, "They profess that they know God; but in works they deny him . . ." (Titus 1:16). Many people say they believe in God but do not live as if God is a reality in their lives. On the other hand, other nominal Christians delude themselves into thinking that if they live good lives they don't need to become real believers. "Having a form of godliness, but denying the power thereof . . ." (2 Timothy 3:5). Both of these groups are usually not consciously aware of their denial.

There is, however, a form of denial that is worthy. As Jesus said to His disciples, "If any man will come after me, let him deny himself, and take up his cross, and follow me" (Matthew 16:24). I have met many missionaries who unconsciously deny the discomforts and difficulties of their lives in the mission field. They are so dedicated to the cause of Christ and serving Him in underdeveloped areas that they become genuinely unaware of the absence of home comforts.

Sublimation consists of attenuating the harmful potential of uncontrollable instinctual drives by diverting their energies into socially acceptable activities. The repressed energy inherent in unacceptable primitive impulses is transformed into actions that promote the cultural development of the individual or his social group. Sexual drives, for example, can be sublimated through such creative activities as hobbies, art, literature, music, sculpturing, design, scientific research, or religion. Aggressive drives are successfully reduced through physical exercise and competitive sports and games. Kolb compares sublimation to the harnessing of the hydrodynamic energy of Niagara Falls. By diverting some of its flow, erosion is reduced and useful electric power is created. Sexual and aggressive drives can also frequently be sublimated by the energetic pursuit of an emotionally and intellectually satisfying job. By contrast, a man not satisfied in his work or career is more likely to find his instinctual drives difficult to control. Sublimation is usually a desirable mechanism as long as a disproportionate amount of time, money, or effort is not spent on the chosen pursuit. Two mechanisms very similar to sublimation are *aim inhibition* and *displacement*.

Aim inhibition consists of the placing of a limitation on an instinctual demand by an unconscious willingness to accept a partial or modified fulfillment of desires. A young Christian couple, becoming aware of mutual sexual desire, will agree that their relationship is only platonic. They verbalize to themselves and to others that they are "just friends" thereby hiding their true feelings from conscious awareness. This is good as a temporary expedient until such time as they decide to get married. Other examples of aim inhibition are: the girl who wanted to become a physician and who, on being rejected from medical school, became a nurse; and the pilot in training who failed due to poor eyesight and settled for being a navigator.

Displacement consists of a change in the object by which an instinctual drive is satisfied. A girl in a church I formerly attended was crushed when her fiancé broke off their engagement. Within a few weeks she announced plans to marry another totally unsuitable, older, divorced man of quite different cultural, ethnic, and educational background. She justified her substitution by saying that he was a better Christian than her former fiancé. Needless to say, this rebound phenomenon resulted in a disastrous and very short-lived marriage.

During World War II, in England when beef was very scarce we ate a lot of whale meat which restaurants called Steak de Jonah! Many others, as well as myself, got used to its rather oily taste and quite enjoyed it. The March Hare in *Alice in Wonderland* said, "I like what I have is the same as I have what I like!" When beef returned in 1946 we didn't like whale meat anymore.

Substitution can cause chain reactions in human relationships. When the harassed employee is reprimanded by his boss he is likely to come home and yell at his wife. She in turn will yell at the kids who may take it out on smaller kids or kick the dog.

Compensation consists of behavior that reduces the effect of inadequacies or imperfections. The most common well-recognized example is the man of short stature who develops aggressive and dominating traits—the Napoleon complex. His deportment makes him feel more secure but his pomposity may result in unpopularity. Compensation can sometimes be valuable if used to develop skills or talents as a reaction to limitations or handicaps. An outstanding example is that of Demosthenes (384–322 B.C.) who overcame physical infirmities, natural weaknesses, and difficult circumstances in his early life to became the greatest orator of the ancient world.

In the context of the Christian experience, the secure personal identity and self-esteem of the man or woman who has Christ as Saviour and Lord can compensate for physical or psychological deficiencies. God made us the way we are—with all our strengths and weaknesses. Knowing our capabilities, He gives us tasks and responsibilities commensurate with them. If my desire is to do God's will in my life He will give me all that I need to enable me to succeed. This will result in emotional and intellectual satisfaction which will obviate the need for compensation. To the church at Philippi, Paul wrote, ". . . I have learned, in whatsoever state I am, therewith to be content. I know both how to be abased, and I know how to abound. . . . I can do all things through Christ which strengtheneth me" (Philippians 4:11–13).

Idealization is an overestimation of the good qualities and under-estimation of the bad points of a desired object. The girl who replaced her lost fiancé with an unsuitable substitute idealized him with the unbalanced view that his Christian maturity would make up for his unattractive points. Unrealistic expectations based on idealization always lead to disappointment.

Reaction formation is an overcompensation for unacceptable impulses by going to the opposite extreme. A married woman in our church found herself becoming attracted to one of her husband's friends. Her Christian principles made her feel so guilty about her feelings that she overreacted by treating the man with cold aloofness. When her actions were explained to her in therapy, the two families once again became friendly. A spinster I know had twice turned down offers of marriage in order to care for her elderly widowed mother. She nursed her with excessive concern and devotion and always spoke of her mother in loving terms. This enabled her to feel less guilty because actually she wished for her death, and had unrecognized feelings of hostility towards her.

Undoing is an attempt to negate the effects of a previous regretted action. A girl I treated felt very guilty about some petting in which she and her boyfriend had indulged. When she next dated him she was very unfriendly toward him. She made no attempt to enjoy their conversation over dinner and refused to let him hold her hand in the movies. In her own mind she was punishing both of them, thereby reducing her guilty feelings, and undoing the damage to her self-concept. When I reminded her that, as Christians, all they had to do was to repent of the extent to which they believed they had sinned, their good relationship was restored.

It is said, as an example of a conscious analogue of *undoing*, that whenever Napoleon had to reprimand an officer he always endeavored at their next meeting to speak some words of praise and appreciation. Small wonder that, by his subordinates, he was one of the most loved of the world's great military leaders.

Dissociation is a splitting of certain thoughts away from the main line of opinion. It can lead to multiple personality, a condition popularized by the movie *The Three Faces of Eve*, in which hidden needs in the real personality were released by acting them out in the form of two other totally different ones. Prejudice within the church is a good example of dissociation. While professing love for all men, many white Christians have disproportionately few black friends and are strongly resistant to the concept of racially mixed marriages, especially if someone in their own family is involved. Their hypocrisy represents a dissociation of their feelings about other ethnic groups from their sincere, conscious ideals about Christian brotherly love and human fellowship.

Fantasy or daydreaming usually represents wishes which are partially or totally unrealistic. They nevertheless provide some measure of pleasure, escape from the stress of a dull, daily routine, and a partial gratification of desires or ambitions which are unattainable. A lady confessed to her pastor that she was troubled with sexual fantasies. He reassured her that temptations were not sins, but exhorted her not to entertain them. "That's not the problem," she said. "The problem is that *they* entertain *me!*"

Daydreaming is detrimental if it occupies too much time or emotional energy. Fantasies of great wealth or power generally detract from living realistically by getting on with one's work or other responsibilities. A girl who daydreams about the perfect boyfriend and refuses to date anyone who does not measure up to her fantasy is being self-destructive in that she will probably be permanently frustrated.

Some fantasies *can* be creative, especially if they have a realistic focus. Golfers have significantly improved their scores by constructively spending time thinking through and meditating on the components of their game. Fantasied situations in which they re-create hypothetical shots in their minds can lead to real improvement on the course. Thinking practically about such things as distance, wind direction, green elevation, slope of the lie, club selection, grip, stance, and swing can lead to these decisions and actions being done correctly and almost automatically when the game is actually in progress.

Dreaming was described by Freud as the royal road to the unconscious. Recent discoveries have shown a sharp difference between deep sleep and shallower dreaming sleep as revealed by quite distinct tracings from the electroencephalograph (EEG) and in the associated existence of rapid conjugate eye movements while dreaming. Dreams represent repressed material and conflicts struggling to achieve recognition. Various mechanisms, such as the use of symbols, effectively disguise dream content. These are hard to correlate with what they represent and therefore dream analysis at best is little better than educated guesswork. Many defense mechanisms are exposed in dreams and may therefore represent attempts on the part of the ego to resolve conflicts, provide wish-fulfilling gratification, and protect from unpleasant effects. It is important to remember that dreams represent a revelation or exposure of what has *previously* entered the mind. In *no* way do dreams foretell the future.

Some psychiatrists regard all neurotic and even some psychotic conditions as outgrowths of basic defensive mental processes. Excluding the not yet clearly defined chemical-imbalance causes of emotional disturbances, they are probably right, at least with regard to the ways in which patients react psychologically to various causative factors.

Finally a reminder: Do not think of these psychological defense mechanisms as being necessarily sinful or unhealthy. Some are, some are not. They need to be evaluated, understood, and controlled. The Christian desiring to do God's will can be given the wisdom and power to deal with them appropriately, and thus live an integrated and balanced life.

PART II

The Family

4

....

EARLY DEVELOPMENT AND
ADULT REGRESSION

For three generations, evangelical Christians have been prejudiced against the teachings of Freud and his followers. One of the reasons for this is that psychoanalytic theory essentially teaches that divergent behavior is merely a departure from the norm, and that a clear understanding of the reasons for the divergence can lead to improvement or at least adaptive change. To the Bible-believing Christian, this is like trying to lift yourself off the ground by pulling up on your own shoelaces. To him, man is inherently sinful, in need, not of self-understanding, but of a Saviour with supernatural power.

Freud said that if you can understand the problem you can deal with it. Jesus said, ". . . for without me ye can do nothing" (John 15:5). Christians also have tended to confuse the psychological and the spiritual. The Freudian analyst regards divergent thought or behavior as a psychological or emotional problem. The Christian tends to see them as a spiritual problem. My contention is that both are partly right. Each of these philosophies has a contribution to make to healing, and therapists using either approach should not only respect the other's viewpoint but attempt where possible to integrate them. In this chapter, use is made of some analytic principles as descriptive guidelines in the consideration of some factors in early development and certain related problems of adult life. An application of each stage to the Christian experience is also attempted.

Development from birth to adult maturity is divided into three

59

periods of approximately seven years each. The first of these septennial periods, which spans infancy and early childhood, is further subdivided into three psychosexual or psychosocial stages: oral, anal, and phallic (oedipal). The second seven-year period is called *latency* and the third, commencing with the onset of puberty, is the *genital or adolescent*. Each stage of development influences the structure of the future adult personality. The individual effects of each one depend on the relative amounts of satisfaction or frustration encountered during it. These stages were first described by Freud.

For example, healthy psychological and emotional development in the young child can be adversely affected by four types of harmful experience: absence of mother or mother-substitute for long periods of time; deflection of parental attention by birth of younger siblings; death of parent, sibling, or other very close family member such as a frequently seen grandparent; serious injury or prolonged physical illness in the child. By contrast, pleasurable and satisfying experiences in these early years will leave many good memories and contribute to a healthy and emotionally stable personality.

The successful passing of a stage does not end the unconscious memory of the various gratifications or pleasures associated with it. There remains a tendency to go back to a fresh experience of the former satisfaction. This is known as *regression* and is an experience to be regarded as within normal limits as long as it does not lead to serious disruptions of functioning efficiency. For example, a five-year-old who returns to thumb-sucking when a sibling is born is manifesting an oral-regressive trait, the rediscovered sucking pleasure compensating for lost parental attention. More serious forms of regression would be the development of bed-wetting, temper tantrums, disobedience, or destructive behavior. (The word *trait* is generally used when the problem is not very serious. The word *regression* is used if the condition is serious enough to warrant treatment of some kind.)

Anytime in life, temporary or prolonged regression may take place under conditions of stress or frustration. A fully mature adult, for example, during a period of physical illness, through demanding dependency, may regress to the point of being burdensome on his wife or the nursing staff. Long-standing regressions in an adult personality can manifest themselves in various neurotic symptoms, or, most seriously of all, in the psychotic thought processes of the schizophrenic.

During the *oral stage,* the first eighteen months of life, the child's main goal-directed behavior is sucking. The first steps towards healthy emotional development and security are taken if the baby is tenderly held, kissed, and caressed with verbal affection during the process of feeding, whether by breast or bottle. Thumb-sucking, investigating his world by means of his mouth, being totally dependent on his mother, and the need for a sense of security derived from warm physical contact are all normal characteristics of this stage. By contrast, even if food supply is good, lack of physical contact can lead to a condition of emaciation called *marasmus,* which in extreme cases can lead to the baby's death.

Towards the end of the oral stage, gradual progress is seen from passive dependence to a more active independence. This process begins with weaning, since the infant is for the first time able to accept or reject alternate foods offered. This represents the first use of the gift of free will. The earliest manifestations of Original Sin will therefore be first recognizable at this stage. Attempts at crawling, then walking, attempts at communication other than by crying, and investigation of his world by sight, hearing, and touch all influence his progress towards maturity. If satisfaction rather than frustration has accompanied physical contact, feeding, and these early attempts at independence, then the child's psychosexual development will have started well. In this case, ego functioning in dealing with his environment, and superego development through identification with parental expectations, will have become firmly established in the right direction.

In the adult, oral regression is manifested in any of the following ways: overeating, finicky undereating, chewing gum, smoking, nail-biting and the excessive use of coffee, tea, or alcohol. More serious adult manifestations of oral regression are passive dependency on other people's assistance, the constant need for affection or encouragement from others to maintain inner security, excessive need for physical contact, or the opposite, being repelled by human touch. A man who feels insecure or is pessimistic about his social or vocational prospects might regress to oral gratification in alcohol to bring him comfort and escape from reality. This only worsens his prospects. Women who are lonely and feel unloved often seek compensation in the pleasure of overeating. This leads to obesity and the vicious circle of lowered self-esteem, leading to more loneliness.

Little can be done to reverse oral regression in a child. He will inevitably grow out of it sooner or later. It can be prevented, however, if care is taken to avoid its causes. For example: when a new baby is born into a family, the parents, especially the mother, must make special efforts to give attention to the next youngest child, the one who would otherwise be the most affected. Oral regression in an adult can sometimes be conquered by sheer self-will and motivation. Both my parents suddenly and completely gave up smoking after over thirty years of indulging at the rate of two or three packs per day. Of course, professional help is needed if the problem has become of such proportions as to have caused serious personal discomfort or loss of performance—as in the case of chronic alcoholism.

The Christian with oral regression misuses the basically sound principle: Let go and let God. He goes to the extreme of dependency, whereby he does nothing to help himself and ascribes all his failures to God's chastening. He relies on other Christians to help him with his financial problems and he becomes a burden on whatever church he joins. The Christian life is a call to service: "Not slothful in business; fervent in spirit; serving the Lord" (Romans 12:11).

The problem is one of motivation and enthusiasm: trusting the Lord but also getting on with the job that has to be done. "I beseech you therefore, brethren . . . that ye present your bodies a living sacrifice, holy, acceptable unto God, which is your *reasonable* service" (Romans 12:1—*italics* added). Some modern translations have used the expressions *rational, spiritual,* or *intelligent* service. Whichever is preferred, the main issue is that God expects of Christians their wholehearted personal dedication to His service.

In his own strength, neither the healthy nor the sick Christian can give this. In the power of the Holy Spirit he *can*. It is appropriate to be dependent on God: "For in him we live, and move, and have our being . . ." (Acts 17:28). The Christian who depends on others without trusting the Lord is often manifesting regression. The Christian who depends on the providence of God is thereby empowered to be "mighty through God to the pulling down of strong holds" (*see* 2 Corinthians 10:4).

The **anal stage,** usually lasting to about the third birthday, is that in which toilet training is the major achievement. Two and a half years is an average age for this to be completed, but parents should not strive for quicker results or worry about delayed ones. Although second and later children, learning from the first, might achieve this more quickly, remember that they will be successful only when their muscles are capable of controlling the bladder and bowels. Parental efforts to hurry the process because of their own inconvenience can harm the child emotionally. There is the immediate danger that he will attempt to express his resentment or hostility by withholding or producing at the wrong times. Worse, there is a later tendency to develop problems with authority figures, or to become an obsessional or compulsive personality. Adult character traits which may derive from the anal stage are:

1. Neatness and cleanliness—or untidiness or dirtiness at the other extreme
2. Problems in obeying orders or in dealing with subordinates who rely on authoritarian leadership
3. Tendency to react to frustration by hostility or destructiveness
4. Obsessional concern over bowel function
5. Stinginess or compulsively accurate bookkeeping—or the opposite: excessive generosity with money ("filthy lucre")
6. Obsessions with deadlines, schedules, and promptness

The Christian with an anal-regression problem tends to see God as a very demanding authority figure instead of a God of forgiveness and love. He strives for spiritual perfection and is depressed when he fails. He tends to be more concerned with the letter of the law than the spirit of it. He is likely to make personal additions to the law to impose upon himself, and possibly his family, in order to obtain a sense of security. Such additions are invariably not scriptural, but cultural. For example, I once knew a church elder who refused to let his wife wear any cosmetics, forbade his children to go to movies, never allowed the radio or television to play on Sundays, and taught his family that the marks of a good Christian were that he didn't smoke, drink, dance, gamble, or swear. He felt secure under God, maintaining all these negative standards himself, but became pathetically shocked when his teen-age children later rebelled. He had forgotten Paul's charge to Timothy to trust "in the living God who giveth us richly all things to enjoy" (*see* 1 Timothy 6:17).

Jesus' admonitions against the Pharisees were not because of their lack of sincerity in maintaining the standards of the Ten Commandments, but because their sect had created over the previous century many man-made extras which had become more important than the Mosaic Law itself. Christians likewise should base their lives solidly on the Scriptures, *not* on cultural or church traditions which historically have been so vulnerable to human error, ignorance, or selfishness. As conservative evangelical or fundamentalist Christians, let us search ourselves in humble prayer to evaluate just how much our life-styles are influenced by our own tradition or upbringing, and how much is genuinely based on the inspired Word of God.

For the Christian, the answer to the anal-regression problem of authority is to remember that God is more willing to forgive than to punish. His love is stronger than His wrath because His love is unfettered, whereas His wrath is tempered with patience, understanding, and mercy. "Like as a father pitieth his children, so the Lord pitieth them that fear him. For he knoweth our frame; he remembereth that we are dust" (Psalms 103:13, 14). We cannot do anything good by ourselves. God's command, "Be ye holy; for I am holy" (1 Peter 1:16) demands a close daily walk with Jesus who ". . . is made unto us wisdom, and righteousness, and sanctification, and redemption" (1 Corinthians 1:30). This daily walk grows out of a love relationship involving obedience to the promptings of the Holy Spirit and the knowledge of His will.

We are living in the Age of Grace, in which our imperfections are covered by the shed blood of the Lamb, but also in which we are called to "be not conformed to this world: but be ye transformed by the renewing of your mind, that ye may prove what is that good, and acceptable, and perfect, will of God" (Romans 12:2). *Perfection* in Scripture means not *sinlessness,* but total yieldedness to the power of God working in us and through us to produce the outworking of His will.

The *phallic stage* of development, from ages three through seven, is the period in which the child becomes aware of male-female differences and discovers increasingly pleasurable sensations from his genital organs. He becomes more fully aware of his own sexual identity through comparison with his parent of the same sex. At the same time he awakens to a much expanded and meaningful relationship with the parent of the opposite sex. This is known as the Oedipus complex in boys, the name being derived from Sophocles' tragedy *Oedipus Rex,* in which the young prince unwittingly kills his father, king of Thebes, and marries his mother. In girls, it is called the Electra complex after the daughter of King Agamemnon, who, with her brother Orestes, killed their mother Clytemnestra.

The essential problem is one of competition. The child competes with the parent of the same sex for the other, and as a result is sometimes fearful of retaliation. Castration anxiety in boys and penis envy in girls are examples of fantasied punishments. Natural curiosity in young children about their sexual organs leads to varying types of parental response. Disapproval or punishment following genital exposure or autoerotic stimulation can lead to feelings of guilt associated with *any* sexual expression. A healthier reaction would be to explain at the child's comprehension level that sex is not dirty but beautiful, but that nevertheless its enjoyment is more appropriate at certain times and under certain conditions than at others.

In particular, even a six-year-old can be expected to understand not only some of the basic principles of the anatomy and physiology of human reproduction but also some of the moral and ethical principles involved. This is not too young an age to teach him that sexual expression is connected with propagation of the next generation, and that this act is very much under the blessing and providence of God when it is done within the context of a marriage commitment between two parents who desire to nurture a family.

It is normal for children up to about the age of seven to want to climb into bed with their parents. They obtain a warm feeling of comfort and security in this and it is a harmless experience as long as care is taken to avoid genital contact. Whereas there is usually no harm in young children seeing their parents naked, it is generally undesirable for them to witness sexual intercourse. This experience, known as the "primal scene," might be misinterpreted as being an act of aggression. The oedipal situation is usually resolved at about the age of seven with normally increased identification with the parent of the same sex.

Adult character traits derived from the phallic stage include primarily those concerned with sexuality, curiosity, and competitiveness. Attitudes towards sex such as guilt, fear or shame, and emotional concomitants such as affection and love, or aggression and lust, are usually the result of experiences at the phallic stage. So also are such attitudes as modesty or exhibitionism, and concepts of other adults as being either objects for admiration and emulation, or for lustful use. Certain adult sexual problems such as impotence, frigidity, perversions, and sexual anxiety may have their roots in these early years.

Early sexual curiosity can sometimes influence later interests in learning, research work, exploration, and a general drive to discover the unknown. Competitiveness or lack of it in adult boy-girl relationships is also an indirect result of phallic-stage experiences. Feelings of jealousy, fear, rivalry and hostility may stem from this. The ruthless businessman, or the tennis player who hates to lose is often found to have unresolved oedipal problems. Generally speaking, however, a reasonable degree of competitiveness in business or sports is necessary for success and can effectively sublimate drives which might otherwise find outlets in other less socially acceptable activities.

The Christian has special problems in the area of phallic regression because of the strict injunctions in Scripture against sexual acting out, and the teaching that only sex within holy matrimony is the highest and most beautiful expression of human functioning. (*See* chapters 9, 12, 13.) Curiosity and competitiveness, however, if controlled within scriptural standards of behavior, can be a great asset to the development of strong, stable, and godly qualities in a Christian.

Tragic or painful experiences in early years can leave permanent scars on a young child's memory and are likely to affect the smoothness of his passage through the particular psychosexual stage he is in when they happen. Probing into real or imagined painful events of early years resurrects from the deep unconscious mind forgotten, but still destructively active, memories which have contributed to regressive tendencies. Therefore, regression problems in adult life can often be eradicated or at least considerably reduced by psychotherapy.

Helping the patient verbalize these memories brings them into conscious awareness. On the strict condition that the patient *wants* to change his unhealthy traits or regressions, he can usually do so once he understands their origins and effects. However, it may not be easy. The true Christian has an additional resource which he can daily appropriate by faith. He has available to him the healing power of the Holy Spirit which can change him and free him from residual feelings of guilt.

The Christian experience lived within biblical principles can be of great influence in both the child (in enhancing healthy development) and in the adult (in maintaining good habits and patterns of behavior). For example, the personal spiritual experience in a child of accepting Jesus as Saviour and Lord of his life will significantly influence his learning of good moral principles. This experience will also give him a desire to become obedient to Christ and seek God's will instead of his own throughout his life. This is especially so if his parents are approving and encouraging. Parents should not underestimate the impact of the simple Gospel message on a preschool child. If, to the emotional warmth of a loving home, is added the awareness by all members of the family that God is

watching over them, protecting, and providing for them, the child
will be doubly blessed. He will grow up, not only with a good
sense of security, but also with a clear awareness of a purpose in
life and a personal identity in the Kingdom of God on earth.

The adult Christian also has these blessings. Appropriating unto
himself the forgiveness available in the shed blood of Christ leads
to a freedom from guilt and a healing of painful memories. As a
new creation in Christ, ". . . old things are passed away; behold,
all things are become new" (2 Corinthians 5:17). Not only does
the new creation know he is being forgiven daily, but he is also
given the spiritual power to forgive all who have harmed him. In
this way he not only loses his burden of guilt—he can also confess
and be cleansed of his bitterness, resentment, jealousy, and hostility
towards others. The Christian experience then, by providing both
forgiveness and power, can greatly enhance the healing process.
These resources, combined with a willingness to change, can lead
both to increased love, joy, and peace within, and also to improved
relationships with loved ones and friends.

Latency: The Happy Years of Character Foundation

"I can't stand girls," said a ten-year-old boy in my office recently.
"They're all sissies!" Distressed though his parents were at his apparent hostility, I quickly pointed out to them that much of his
attitude could be explained by the fact that he was going through
a normal stage of human development in which interest in the
opposite sex is at an all-time low.

This is the period which psychoanalysts call *latency*, a word
which means a state of quiescence or lying dormant. Anyone with
a ten-year-old boy at home knows that he is far from quiet or
dormant. The word refers to the relative inactivity of the sexual
drive between the usual end of the oedipal period and the onset
of puberty. The energy of this drive, however, is not wasted, but
displaced into the child's most important function at this time—
learning. What he learns during this period lays the foundation
for the kind of character he will have as an adult.

During latency, sexual interests, though reduced, do not disappear completely. In fact, while the child seeks after the parent or friends of the opposite sex during the early and late periods of development, during this middle period he develops friendships of the same sex. The parent of the same sex becomes the prime focus of identification and emulation. This is the normal homosexual time in a person's life, and therefore the time in which loss of the parent of the same sex, through death or divorce, can be a disaster to future healthy psychosexual development. (*See* chapter 9.) Hero worship by boys or "having a crush" by girls may be regarded as normal and healthy. The establishment of a sense of masculinity or femininity often results from a real or imagined friendship with an admired older friend of the same sex.

From first grade onward, groups or gangs tend to form and a healthy result of these is the development of ideals, ambitions, and standards of behavior acceptable to others. Whereas the preschool child is usually occupied with things of individual interest, the latency child becomes progressively more socialized. He begins to be able to share unselfishly and to play in team games. The more mature he becomes, the more he is concerned for the success of the team rather than for himself. Concepts of cooperation, compromise, taking turns, and contributing his part for the good of the whole are developed. He learns to play fair and to abide by the discipline of the rules of the game. Outstanding signs of increasing maturity are his ability to be patient, to wait for postponed gratification, and to be willing to put the interests of other individuals or his group above himself.

Latency is also a happy carefree time when the child is old enough to explore and appreciate many of the good and exciting things in his world, yet not old enough to have the anxieties and frustrations of the teen-age years. His mind is developed to the point where he is stimulated and aroused by new learning experiences, and he therefore needs to be taught to discern between good and bad, safe and dangerous, and socially acceptable or unacceptable. During this period he also acquires an early sense of identity and develops his first conscious sense of self-worth. Indeed, one of the fundamental principles of good character foundation is the establishment at this time of a healthy self-concept which will carry through later to become the basis for all his future inter-personal relationships. This ego development and the basic cultural skills he needs to acquire come preeminently from his identification with his parents and teachers, on whom, therefore, the responsibility for these achievements largely rests.

Between the ages of nine and twelve a child is most receptive to discussions on moral and religious issues. Earlier, he will have only limited understanding; later his blooming adolescent mind will tend to become confused with intellectual arguments. Given help from his parents or Sunday-school teachers, a latency-age child will not only learn from, but actually enjoy, reading the Scriptures and praying. He can thereby acquire additional resources to influence the development of a solid foundation for the character he will have as an adult.

5

SOME PRINCIPLES OF RAISING
YOUNG CHILDREN

Many books have been written on how to raise children. All of them can be summed up in one verse from the Bible: "Train up a child in the way he should go: and when he is old, he will not depart from it" (Proverbs 22:6). This truth, written about 3,000 years ago, probably by King Solomon, has remained the cornerstone of the building of every human character throughout the centuries. The fundamental fact involved is that if the basic principles of right and wrong, of good and bad, of truth and deceit, of love and selfishness, and of reward and punishment, can be impressed clearly on the small child's earliest memories he will carry with him throughout his life a deeply ingrained concept of appropriate standards of behavior, and an acutely tuned conscience. The poet Wordsworth wrote, "The Child is father of the Man," meaning that good or bad qualities developed in childhood directly influence the character produced in adult life.

If, to good moral principles, is added a personal commitment to Jesus Christ as Saviour and Lord, an individual decision which can be made with full awareness and understanding as early as the age of four or five, the developing child will have the additional resource of the power of the Holy Spirit to help him deal with all the decisions and temptations he will be confronting, not only through childhood years but for the whole of his adult life. It is the parents' responsibility to teach their children these basic principles and to lead them to the point where they clearly understand the things of God. They will then be able to make their own decisions on yielding to the authority of Christ as King in their lives. Be careful, however, that God the Father is presented not only as an authority figure but also as a God of love, understanding, forgiveness and providence. If this is done, there will be far less likelihood of children of strictly religious parents rebelling in adolescent years.

Children are widely dissimilar from birth. Hereditary and congenital factors influence such characteristics as intelligence, temperament, emotional stability, and physical appearance and abilities. In spite of these differences most children quickly learn to adapt to the needs of healthy living in a stressful and even dangerous world. Spiritual awareness is also inherently present in most children and they are therefore wide open to religious influences, good or bad, from parents and other adults. The longer a young child lives in a godly home the greater are his chances of embracing for himself a personal faith similar to that of his parents. The longer a child is deprived of basic religious instruction the less likely he is to understand or be influenced by it in adult years. God intervenes, miracles happen, and pagans are converted through the faithful witness of believers; but generally such converts have at some point in early life received spiritual influences which, after years of lying dormant, reach fruition when the Gospel is heard.

Let us now consider some of the specific responsibilities that Christian parents should exercise in order to give their children a good upbringing.

Love

Love must be outwardly expressed, not only constantly toward the children, but also between the parents in front of the children. One of the greatest factors in the development of emotional security in a child is seeing his parents hold hands, kiss and hug, and in many ways show their affection and love for one another.

Love is patient; love is kind and envies no one. Love is never boastful, nor conceited, not rude; never selfish, not quick to take offence. Love keeps no score of wrongs; does not gloat over other men's sins, but delights in the truth. There is nothing love cannot

face; there is no limit to its faith, its hope, and its endurance. Love
will never come to an end . . . .

1 Corinthians 13:4–8 NEB

This divinely inspired description of love from the Bible can be
applied point by point in the Christian home.

For example, parents of small children should frequently during
each day hold them close, talk with them at their level, and play
with them, either with their toys or by simply romping on the
floor. They must not allow their own worries and problems to
become a barrier to this kind of closeness. Nor should presents or
material gifts become substitutes for love. Love should be demon-
strated by attention and verbal expressions of affection. Children
who are loved and know they are loved and can grow up in a
home in which this is an unchanging reality for them and for their
parents, will turn into secure and emotionally mature adolescents
and adults. They will be able to relate to others in all their interpersonal relationships with self-assurance and confidence and will
one day be able to provide homes in which their own children can
also grow up to be emotionally stable and personally secure.

Discipline

"A father who spares the rod hates his son, but one who loves
him keeps him in order" (Proverbs 13:24 NEB). Notice in these
words of wisdom that love and discipline are brought together.
The word *rod* does not necessarily imply spanking, though this is
sometimes needed. Some important points about discipline should
be made.

A child must always be disciplined in love. This means that punishment for wrongdoing must be meted out in such a way that the
child understands that his transgression in no way affects his parents' love for him. Indeed, discipline itself is an act of love imposed
so that the child might benefit and become a better person.

The goal of punishment is correction—teaching improved conduct.
Self-will needs to be tamed and brought into subjection. With careful leadership, parents can help the child achieve this without
damaging a healthy self-image. Every child is entitled to under-

stand clearly why he is being punished. Explanation, at his level of understanding, as to why he is being spanked, must accompany the act. Point out that rules have reasons. Explain that self-control and self-discipline are cardinal qualities of the future mature adult. Even a young child is entitled to opinions. Take these seriously, even if you believe them to be wrong. Help him to understand the reasoning behind your point of view. In this way, he will comprehend better and be less likely to make the same mistake again.

Punishment should be for disobedience—not for ignorance or accidents. Parents must teach their children the expected standards of behavior, and maintain those standards by discipline. Do not punish a transgression perpetrated because the child did not know that it was wrong. Do not punish for the genuine accident, even if partially blameworthy. Remember that young children are relatively uncoordinated and accidents will happen. Forgive, explain, and clearly warn of punishment the next time. Teach him to respect other people's property rights and to be unselfish and thoughtful of others.

Never strike a child through your own impatience or exasperation or as a reaction to your own worrisome problems. A spanking should be done with emotional control and within the principles of "due process of law"—never as an impulsive frustrated retaliation to vent explosive feelings or to achieve a satisfied feeling of revenge. On the other hand, mothers should deal with disobedience quickly and not say, "Wait till your father comes home." Parents should act consistently and agree on discipline principles. Never let a child play one parent against the other. If successful, he may feel insecure.

Standards must be clearly set and maintained. Reasonable degrees of flexibility are of course necessary but the child must know where he stands, and the limits set. He becomes insecure if he finds that overstepping the known limits are not immediately and appropriately dealt with, in the manner in which he has previously been warned. There is the additional danger that this insecurity will be compounded later with a lack of respect for his parents when he becomes old enough to realize the inconsistencies in their standards.

Mode and severity of punishment should not be unreasonable. Excessive punishment can lead to lying, through fear, and can cause serious inhibition of the healthy self-expression which is such an essential part of personality development. Avoid saying, "You are a bad boy"; or "You make me unhappy when you do this." This may develop either a poor self-image or sense of guilt. Deprivation of some pleasure or privilege is sometimes more severe than a spanking because it lasts longer, and it might be more appropriate to a particular "crime." Deprivation is usually more appropriate in older children. Spanking should be administered on the rear end and nowhere else, to avoid injury. In a small child use a slipper, rolled-up magazine, or similar harmless object for spanking, rather than the hand. The young child will then tend to equate the slipper with punishment. He should learn to equate his parents' hands not with pain, but with giving and holding and loving.

After each punishment forgive and forget. Never bring up the subject once it has been dealt with. Reassure the child of your continued love. This and your forgiveness will be nonverbal examples to your children of God's grace towards us.

In disobedience situations be calm but firm. Let reprimands, whenever possible, be in private, not in front of houseguests. Try not to blame one child rather than another, even if only one seems to be to blame: young children usually get into trouble *together*. Avoid comparing one child adversely with another in an individual situation; but especially do not let one child feel that he is always the one in the wrong. Be strictly fair and equal to all the children in discipline or punishment problems.

Remember you are a parent not a pal. A child needs pals, but he usually has plenty of them in school, church, or youth activities. He only has two parents to admire, respect, and emulate. Parents dilute or even destroy their roles as leaders, teachers, and inspirers if they do not maintain a balanced authority gap. A parent is authority with forgiveness, flexibility, and understanding; conscience with reason, discipline, and love.

Communication and Approachability

As the child grows, it becomes increasingly important to develop genuine two-way communication between him and his parents. "Don't do that—because I say so!" is the worst form of communication because it is strictly one-way. We parents must listen to the child's opinions and humble ourselves to be patient enough to try to understand his point of view. We must respect his opinion and explain why we believe ours is a better course of action and present it to him logically at his level of understanding so that he has a chance to see the alternative viewpoint. By contrast, it is occasionally necessary to be authoritative without explanation. This happens, for example, when the child is using the question *Why?* as an intellectual game with which he attempts to manipulate his parents to his will. In such cases, do not feel guilty for being firm. Don't use baby talk. Speak as an adult. He'll learn more quickly.

If communication is two-way with regard to matters of discipline, it will be invaluable in the meeting of the child's personal and emotional needs. There should be a transparency in the parent-child relationship which permits either to speak freely with the other. It is tragic to hear a young person say, "I can't talk to my parents about it." A major factor in ensuring a sense of security in a child is his knowledge from experience that no matter what happens to him in any area of life, he can talk to his mother or father about it. Both must be approachable to talk about any subject—problems in school, exams, studies, sports, future college or career, money, friends, social activities, dating, sex, and any other emotional or intellectual problems. The secure and mature child or adolescent will be one who can immediately turn first to his own home for help when he is confronted with any unexpected disappointment or need for advice, reassurance, or encouragement.

Part of good communication and approachability is for parents to share responsibilities and family decisions with all their children. There are many little chores around the house, garage, or yard for which children can be made responsible. Doing their share gives them a sense of achievement and self-worth. Responsibility leads to maturity, fills many idle moments away from trouble, and makes the child feel an integral part of the family. Avoid undue pressure or too high an expectation for his stage of development. This can lead to defiance, guilt, loss of interest, and nervous habits like nail-biting, daydreaming, and bed-wetting.

Decision-making, with all family members involved, is also important. Even a three-year-old can be allowed to choose, with adult guidance, what clothes he will wear and what food he will eat. The offer of appropriate choices leads to a sense of responsibility. How to spend a weekend or where to go on a trip or vacation are all family decisions that children should be able to share.

Time

Both parents should impose self-discipline upon themselves with respect to their own routines. Time should be scheduled to be spent with the children. Even if communication and approachability are good, the child or adolescent needs to know that he can spend time regularly with both his parents on particular occasions. A father must especially organize his evening and weekend activities so that he can be doing things frequently and regularly with his children. He will not be able to maintain adequate communication and approachability if he progressively becomes a stranger to them as they grow up. Further, he is the first adult male with whom they will identify as they develop, and their concept of him will distinctly color their image of what a man should be like. This demands time spent together, doing things together; not merely cohabiting in the same house.

Mothers also, especially for their younger children, must organize their household duties and other obligations so that they can play with them frequently during the day. Childhood passes all too rapidly. Those precious years must be filled with all the attention both parents can give them. This attention, however, should not consist mainly of scolding, controlling, and disciplining. Attention means doing with them what *they* want to do, and showing enjoyment in sharing in their play. However bored you may become with their little games, do be willing to sacrifice time to give them the thrill of having your undivided interest. The joy and benefit a child derives from those few precious minutes when he has his parent all to himself far outweighs the temporary inconvenience to the parent of having to delay other duties. Enjoy your child, and he will enjoy and cherish those minutes which make his life so fulfilling.

Instruction

Parents must teach—it is not only the responsibility of the school-teacher. In school the child learns the facts he needs to know to become an educated person, and is instructed in certain mental or mechanical skills which can enable him to obtain good employment when he grows up. In the home the child is instructed in those qualities of life which enable him to develop an attractive personality, a stable temperament, and a reliable and upright character. At home he is taught the right way to do things and gently led to learn by his mistakes. We learn much more quickly and sometimes more thoroughly if we are taught the right way *before* having a chance to make the mistakes. Moral and religious principles should be taught primarily in the home, not at school, or even in church. All the facts of sex he needs to know at a particular age should come to him first from his mother and father, and his parents are preeminently responsible for ensuring that he knows right from wrong in this and all other areas of life.

Example

Actions speak louder than words. How true this is in the whole area of parent-child relationships! If parents spend time with their children they can teach them many things just by simply doing things together. The quality of parents' lives directly influences the child. Honesty, truthfulness, righteous living, keeping promises, maintaining moral principles and ethical standards in all practices, and communicating these virtues by deeds as well as words will give strength and consistency to the developing conscience of the child.

Consider two important problem areas: lying and stealing. There is no point in teaching a child not to tell lies if you do the same in front of him on the telephone or in the company of guests. Telling him not to steal is valueless if he later learns that you are not declaring all your income or overclaiming deductions on your income tax returns. By example, parents can also inspire enthusiasm in a wide variety of interests and activities. Instruction and help with hobbies and encouragement in sports and other indoor and outdoor pursuits can expand horizons and make childhood years exciting and satisfying. This alone will prevent much of the boredom of affluence which leads so often to delinquent behavior in later years. The foundations of a good adult character are laid not only with talk but also with example; not only with teaching, but also with living.

The Family Altar

This is the tradition which makes a Christian home significantly different from one in which Christ is not honored. The theocratic hierarchy is clearly taught in Scripture: Christ is the Lord of the home, the husband and father the human spiritual leader under Christ, and the wife and children in subjection and obedience to him in that order. In our generation, subjection and obedience do not mean inferior status and servitude. The meaning is that it is the Christian duty of the father of the family to take on the obligation of spiritual leadership in the home. This in no way negates equality of husband and wife. It is not a matter of who is the boss. It is a matter of sharing various responsibilities. (*See* chapter 11.)

Paul wrote: "Children, obey your parents in the Lord: for this is right. Honour thy father and mother . . . . And, ye fathers, provoke not your children to wrath: but bring them up in the nurture and admonition of the Lord" (Ephesians 6:1, 2, 4).

The ideal Christian home is one in which all members love and serve Christ as their own Lord. Where Christian love and worship of the Lord are the dominant features in the home, the marriage between parents is joyful, peaceful, and mutually satisfying, and the children are nurtured in security and love. Family prayers with Bible reading is the central act of worship. The whole Scripture should be studied systematically and repeatedly over the years so that the Word of God soaks permanently into the minds and hearts of all members of the family. Parents should teach their children how to come to know Christ personally. They should pray *for* their children and *with* their children, mentioning each one individually by name. Children should be taught to intercede for each other, for their parents, family, and friends and to make supplication for their own needs in conformity with God's will for their lives. Repentance, praise, and giving of thanks for all things prevent self-centeredness in their prayers.

Homes in which the love of Christ fills every heart will be homes in which the Holy Spirit will be able to control, inspire, and guide every member and give power to resist temptation and to live godly lives. This is not an unrealistic ideal. It is the practical reality of a genuine spirituality in many homes today, where submission to Christ has resulted in His loving care for every member, protection from outside danger, and security, fulfillment, peace, and happiness within their walls.

6

....

UNWED PREGNANCY AND
OTHER PROBLEMS OF ADOLESCENCE

One of the most satisfying parts of my job as a practicing psychiatrist in New York City are my regular visits to the Heartsease Home, a Christian haven for unwed pregnant girls. These young ladies, usually in their teens, spend the last two or three months of their pregnancy at Heartsease away from their families, schools, or jobs, and it is my privilege during their stay to talk with all of them about their lives and backgrounds. In spite of the recent availability of legal abortions, there remain many unwed girls who choose to carry their pregnancies to term—for either personal, financial, medical, moral, or religious reasons. They are suddenly and unexpectedly faced with adult responsibility and are forced to mature rapidly. They are emotionally vulnerable during this time in their lives and for this very reason are often more open to the Christian Gospel than at other times. These girls, often their parents, and sometimes also the responsible unwed fathers are in need of advice, sympathy, and understanding from family, friends, social agencies, and professional counselors. Over the years I have learned many things from them which I want to share, in the expectation that some of what I have discovered can be of help to parents.

Many sincere Christian couples naïvely assume that their homes will automatically be good ones in which to raise their families. Tragically, this is often not the case. Several of the girls I have seen have come from Christian homes and they were as bitter about their parents as the others. Although out-of-wedlock pregnancies have been the main focus of my investigations, the facts I have discovered and the opinions shared by these basically healthy young girls can be applied to any home in which young people are either in conflict with their parents or under pressure from their friends. Hopefully, this chapter will be of interest and help not only to families with an unwed-pregnancy problem, but to all Christian parents of teen-age girls or boys. It is possible also that inasmuch as the unwed mother is now herself a parent some thoughts here might be of help to her as well.

Sometimes the girls were able to explain why they became pregnant, from their own self-understanding and insight. At other times, intense but gentle questioning by me helped them to verbalize things they had never before been able to share with a caring adult. Almost all admitted that their pregnancy was not an accident completely outside their conscious control. Most of the girls' pregnancies were the result of one or more of the following dozen causes:

Ignorance   Simple ignorance of the basic facts of life is by far the most common immediate cause of conception. Well over half the girls I have talked with did not have a clear understanding of the fundamentals of the menstrual cycle. Their knowledge of the physiology of ovulation and fertilization was extremely vague. Their planning on the so-called safe period was founded not on medical facts but on a consensus of opinion from their friends who possessed equal or greater ignorance. One or two girls, prior to becoming pregnant, did not even realize the connection between sexual intercourse and human reproduction. In this whole category I hold the girls' parents completely responsible. It is unequivocally the parents' duty to teach their sons and daughters the facts of sex as soon as they are old enough to understand them, and absolutely no later than the arrival of puberty. This responsibility should not be delegated to the local family physician, pastor, priest, or rabbi, nor to sex education in the schools, nor worst of all, to the child's own friends and playmates.

Inadequate Contraception   This is also a matter of ignorance for which parents are responsible. In the case of a Christian family, however, parents sometimes deliberately avoid the subject of contraceptive techniques for fear that by teaching them they would actually be condoning premarital sex by their teen-agers. It does not necessarily follow that to give this essential instruction in any way implies covert approval of extramarital indulgence. Indeed, parents must emphasize the opposite. They should teach their children about contraception as part of their total sex instruction, including such issues as population control, so that they can have complete knowledge to the extent necessary for them—certainly so that they might be no more ignorant than their non-Christian friends. Imparting information about contraceptives does not imply approval of their use outside marriage and this must be made clear.

An important argument in this area is that if at some future date their children *do* choose to become involved in premarital sexual relations, it is the lesser of two evils that they should have purchased and used contraceptive devices rather than to have caused the greater evil of an unwanted pregnancy.

Christian parents who anticipate or experience difficulty or anxiety for any reason in their attempts to teach the basic facts of contraception to their children should first consult both their pastor and their family physician for advice and practical suggestions. However, the actual responsibility of teaching the children *must* remain with the parents.

Inadequate Moral Teachings   Clearly a vitally important part of sex education is the necessity for moral and spiritual principles to be impressed upon the child from the very earliest age. Committed Christians believe that fornication and adultery are sins to be strictly avoided. Surprisingly, even some of these girls from Christian homes had never been taught this. Healthy sexual relations can only be enjoyed with full emotional satisfaction, and without guilt, within the mutually committed and permanent relationship of marriage. Many of the girls at Heartsease had little or no understanding of the concept of sin as an inherited human tendency. Some had no appreciation that the proper use of their bodies was subject to the limits of absolute standards of right and wrong. They hear of immoral behavior from their friends. They are exposed to it in movies, television, reading matter, and advertisements and

grow up thinking that what they see is normal and socially acceptable behavior.

Quite apart from religious principles, their parents are the ones
primarily responsible for counteracting these bad influences. Of
course, some non-Christian parents also fulfill this responsibility—
it is not only a religious matter. Many families which make no
profession or practice of personal religion nevertheless hold to certain basic ethical and moral principles for the good, both of the
individual and society as a whole.

It is clear that sexual license usually leads eventually to disappointment, guilt, frustration, and emotional pain in one or both
parties involved. Christian parents teaching their children should
emphasize these personal and social dangers and not just state
dogmatically that extramarital sex is forbidden simply because the
Bible says so. They should also carefully correlate Christian moral
principles with other teachings of the Old and New Testaments
and properly integrate the ideal of clean living with the larger
concept of yielding oneself totally to Christ for the purpose of
finding and fulfilling His perfect will for one's life. The Christian
young person knows that paying the temporary price of chastity
before marriage is small compared to the peace and joy he or she
experiences both in fellowship with Christ during the waiting
years and in the lifetime of holy marriage that is the later reward.

Too-Early Dating   Amazingly, in our generation parents frequently permit or actually encourage their children to start dating
long before they are mature enough to handle the responsibilities.
Sadly, being pushed into adulthood too quickly almost inevitably
leads to disappointment and heartache. Sometimes parents simply
give in when their children persist in demanding the dating privilege
because of pressure from their friends and a desire for peer-group
acceptance. The parents erroneously believe that they are somehow
depriving their children if they refuse to allow them to experience
the same things as the ones next door. The opposite is the truth.
Many adolescent girls, when they have matured and seen havoc
in their friends' lives, have actually thanked their parents for having
been strict with them during earlier years, and for thereby having

prevented them from becoming involved in situations which they were too young to handle at the time. It is a tragedy to deprive children of a few extra carefree years in which they can consolidate the development of their characters and personalities without the demands of adult responsibility that dating involves. For some parents there is the opposite problem of their own insecurity. Their need to impress their friends by their child's early dating and supposed advanced development is tragically selfish and can only lead to suffering and harm in his or her life.

A final problem in this area is the matter of parents getting vicarious pleasure from their children's dating and sex lives. They obtain some secret satisfaction from seeing their children do what they cannot now do themselves, nor were able to do in their own adolescent years. Such people are often in need of professional counseling or psychiatric treatment.

Too-Little Parental Love   It is not enough to love your children. You must *show them* constantly and demonstrate by your overt affection that they are the objects of your deepest love. This applies to *all* your children. So often if there is favoritism towards one child over the others this can make them feel deprived. By contrast, if one child is less gifted or attractive than the others, this child is in need of added assurance that he is loved as much as the others.

Parents must realize that a young adolescent girl is going through a very delicate period in her physical and psychosexual development. During this period of life, the early teens, she is especially in need of attention and considerate understanding by both her parents. At this period her parents must be aware of the emotional turmoil, the confusion of thoughts and feelings, and the relative instability of moods which are normal for the girl at this stage. Inadequate attention and a lack of demonstration of love can cause her to feel unwanted or unappreciated. Her need for love and approval, if not securely available at home, may be satisfied elsewhere. The attention she gets from a boyfriend at school might begin to fill the void she feels within. If the situation continues and their relationship becomes more intimate she will reach the point of no return where her craving for his love leads to loss of virginity and possible pregnancy.

By contrast, parents who not only deeply love their children, but frequently demonstrate that love by word and action, will enable them to develop through adolescence to adulthood secure in the fact they are wanted and appreciated. The emotional security of a loving home is the greatest single factor in obviating a girl's need to search for satisfaction in superficial and ultimately disappointing relationships outside.

A Bad Home   Some parents actually do not love their children, though this is relatively rare and is usually only found in people who are mentally ill or emotionally disturbed. More often the problem is that they seriously neglect their children's needs. Cruel or physically violent parents, or ones who are so careless, selfish, or thoughtless that the home becomes a nightmare to live in, will force their children to desire to leave as soon as they possibly can. Even in some Christian homes, if the parents are too rigid and demanding and too unwilling to allow reasonable freedoms and privileges there is the danger that the teen-age children will desire to break away. Some Christian parents foolishly pressure their children into regular churchgoing and Sunday-school attendance, hoping that this will cause them to become believers. These children then grow up identifying this rigidity with the church and with the Christian faith. No wonder they leave as soon as they are free to do so!

There are endless reasons why some homes become unhappy, but basic to all the many different particular problems is the fundamental insecurity of the unloved child and his reaction to the miserable situation. A boy might run away, drop out of school, or become involved in illegal drugs and other delinquent or even criminal activities. A girl may become a drug addict or prostitute or become pregnant deliberately to punish her parents and bring shame on the family. Sometimes she will get pregnant in the hope that she will be able to get married early and thereby escape from her intolerable parental home.

A Broken Home   This can lead to serious emotional stress in the adolescent girl. Controlled statistical studies done at the New York Hospital in 1972 showed that women experiencing divorce or death of husband or other very close relative are much more likely to experience stress, leading to unwanted pregnancy as an unconscious means of escape. Even for psychiatrically normal teenagers afflicted with death or divorce of their parents, the exceptional emotional distress this causes them can lead to an unconscious wish for pregnancy as a way of repairing their damaged psyche. They need their "unwanted" babies to prove that they are truly feminine, healthy enough to create, or as a defense against being alone.

The Spoiled Child   The opposite extreme is the overprotective home in which parents give their daughter a very sheltered life, putting her on a pedestal and almost worshiping her. In their efforts to protect her from sin they give her the impression that moral requirements are much higher for her than for her brothers or friends. Unexpected freedom when she goes away to college, plus the peer-group pressure she receives there, influence her to prove to herself and her parents that she is normal and human. The arguments, "Life isn't a Sunday school. . . . Why not relax a bit? . . . A little petting is not that bad," can sway her in a vulnerable moment. The parents' response to her pregnancy is predictable. They put on the martyr act. "Where did we fail? What did we do wrong? We don't deserve this. How could you do this to us?" There has to be a balance. It is needful for moral principles to be accompanied by freedom to pursue healthy and wholesome activities, and by the development of interests and ambitions which can protect and strengthen her normal defenses.

Attempt to Secure Boyfriend   Sometimes a teen-age girl, even from a loving home, falls in love with a boyfriend and is much distressed when she discovers that he is dating another girl. She then fantasizes that if she gets pregnant by him she will thereby force him to give up the other girl and marry her. This technique used to work very well in the nineteenth century when quick marriage was the only way to hush up an out-of-wedlock pregnancy:

but not any more. Abortion is now readily available and is legal in many states. Also, public opinion has changed regarding the so-called shotgun wedding. For any couple to be forced to get married before they are both ready for it is the worst of all possible beginnings to any hoped-for lifetime relationship.

One other factor so often overlooked by the girl is that the desired boyfriend is frequently turned off sexually towards her once he discovers she is pregnant. The burden of anxiety and worry in the boy, coupled with resentment against her for her share of the responsibility, and his feeling of being trapped, is quite enough to cool any love he might have had for her originally.

The Christian girl who is mature enough in her personal faith to trust God's will for her life will be able to deal with the apprehension of the other-girl situation by believing that things will work out for the best in the long run. If she can maintain her conviction that God knows what is best for her and that He will provide His matchless choice of a life partner for her at the right time, she will be able to remain at peace within as she commits her deepest desires and life's plan in surrender to her Lord's loving and perfect will. Christ Himself fills the love void.

Lack of Aims   Some adolescents just hate school and can see no future in striving for good grades or trying to go to college. They frequently come from homes which have underestimated the value of education, emphasized that a woman's destiny is to be a wife and mother, and a man's to get a job as soon as he possibly can. Such people lack personal ambitions, aims, or objectives in life and are very poorly motivated for achieving anything beyond immediate gratification of needs. Life is empty and boring; the future uninspiring or even hopeless.

Empty minds find trouble, and the easiest trouble to find is a relationship with another person of similar shallow objectives. The couple really do not care what happens. Sex becomes one of the few exciting or enjoyable things in an otherwise dull and colorless life. Petting becomes boring or frustrating and a pregnancy develops, either willfully or thoughtlessly. Such young people are urgently in need of counseling and usually their parents could also benefit from some professional help since they are often at least partially responsible.

Drugs Much has been written about marijuana in arguing for its legalization because it is not as physically harmful as, for example, alcohol which is legal. My concern here is not primarily with its legality or medical properties, but with the fact that young people under its influence lose their inhibitions and ability to act with self-control. The ability to resist taking stronger drugs such as LSD, amphetamines, barbiturates, or even heroin is much reduced. The ability to resist becoming involved in a sexual experience is similarly reduced. Healthy, normal, "good" girls who would never submit to taking dangerous drugs or having sex while they were in full possession of their faculties have all too often succumbed at a "pot party."

Pregnancy following a genuine rape is rare, but the young girl whose conscious control has been temporarily weakened by drugs and then submits to sexual intercourse is in fact being raped, at least in the sense that it is happening contrary to her natural volition. Part of sex education, therefore, should include adequate information about the dangers of drugs of any kind, but particularly about alcohol and marijuana because of their specific properties of increasing sexual urges at the same time as diminishing control of the rational mind or conscience.

Thoughtless Exposure Quite apart from taking drugs the sensible girl should try to avoid being trapped into any potentially tempting situation. The backseat of her boyfriend's car is a very easy place for illicit sex on a dark evening down a lonely country lane. So is her own bedroom when her parents are out of the house, or a quiet spot in a park, or on a beach after dark. If her date attempts to persuade her to accompany him into any compromising situation the Christian girl should remember that the easiest time to resist temptation is at the very beginning. She should be taught specifically by her father and mother some of the warning signals, and how tactfully but firmly she can resist them. She can reasonably expect to be treated by her date with the respect due to a lady, and if this respect is not afforded her, she should know from her teaching at home that there will be no lasting pleasure or satisfaction from this type of relationship.

At the youngest age that they can properly comprehend all the implications, children should be instructed by their parents how they should behave on a date and thoroughly warned of the dangers of getting themselves into situations in which the ability to resist temptation is difficult or impossible. God preserved Daniel in the lion's den but Daniel had to cooperate by not putting his head into a lion's mouth!

There are some final points on the dangers of either thoughtless (or deliberate) succumbing to temptation. A boy may try a wide variety of arguments to persuade the girl to give him sexual gratification, not caring about either the physical or emotional after-effects on her. For the Christian girl especially, loss of virginity represents a very permanent and actual physical evidence of sin committed. Though God forgives and forgets after repentance, the damage can never be undone, and to a greater or lesser degree the girl will always feel hypocritical about the symbolism of the "white wedding" which she might hopefully have at a later date.

Along the same line of argument, both for boys and girls, it generally follows that the wider has been the premarital sexual experience, the more difficult it is to remain faithful to one partner after marriage. To the extent that any young person has enjoyed a variety of sexual encounters before marriage, to that same extent will he or she experience dissatisfaction or even boredom with marital fidelity, once the thrill and novelty of the honeymoon has worn off. Conversely, it generally follows that the less sexual experience a person has had before marriage the more satisfied he is likely to be with the one partner he has chosen for a lifetime.

Another argument frequently used is, "We can always get an abortion if worse comes to worst." This is not as easy as it sounds. Much anguish and pain, physical, emotional and financial, are always a part of this procedure, be it done legally or illegally. Shame and guilt will remain permanently in the memories of the couple involved, especially if they believe, as many Christians do, that abortion is murder, thus adding yet another emotional scar to their already lowered self-concept.

A final tragic result to be considered, especially among the promiscuous, is the danger of contracting and spreading venereal disease. The discovery and widespread use of penicillin during and after World War II contributed immensely to wiping out both syphilis and gonorrhea for a time. But now the incidence of these diseases is on the increase again, and statistically the highest age group involved is the late teens and early twenties. There is some evidence that germs causing these diseases have developed a resistance to penicillin and other antibiotics so that treatment is not as simple as it once was. Gonorrhea, unless quickly treated, can cause painful narrowing of the urine passage in males and chronic pelvic disease, possibly leading to infertility in women. Syphilis is even more dangerous. It is more difficult to detect and can lead to permanent damage to the brain, spinal cord and major blood vessels, and premature death.

The best contraceptive device since the beginning of time is the little word *no*. The Christian girl, properly informed and educated, and filled with the power of God's Holy Spirit—given to her when she committed her life to Christ as her Saviour and Lord—is able to say this little word and mean it. By so doing she will be missing out only on a fleeting self-destructive, guilt-inducing moment of temporary gratification. She will be gaining by contrast the continuing peace and joy of communion with her Lord, respect for herself, and the assurance that both now and always her reward will be God's best provision for all her needs.

PART III

Youth

7

....

EMOTIONAL PROBLEMS OF YOUTH

After leaving his relatively protected parental home the young person in his late teens or early twenties finds himself quite suddenly faced with adult responsibilities for which he is often unprepared. It comes as quite a shock, for example, to a freshman just arrived at college to realize that he is now on his own and responsible for his own destiny. He finds that poor grades can seriously jeopardize his future career and that bad behavior can bring rejection by his peers or expulsion from school. He had previously taken much for granted, his parents having supplied all his needs, but now he is a separate individual with a unique personality and this very fact can cause him much anxiety as he ponders many questions: What am I doing here? Who am I? What is my true identity? How do I develop a balanced self-esteem? What is the meaning of maturity? How can I be sure I will be making correct career decisions for myself?

Identity

I worked for almost three years in psychiatric clinics which specialized in the treatment of college students in the New York area. Students often came to see us not because they were mentally ill but because they were searching for some answers to questions regarding their own identity. They were trying to find themselves, to sort out what was authentic about themselves and what was false. They wanted to come to grips with the "real me." They desperately wanted to be honest and to avoid hypocrisy. For the most part, they were aware of their youthful vulnerability to the powerful influences to which they were subjected, and they were therefore very anxious that they should be able quickly to discern those which were helpful to them in their development and those which were destructive.

Many a college freshman has been to see me with the request that I help him to find his own authentic self and to realize his true identity. He never puts the question in quite this way, of course, but I soon perceive as he is telling me about his problems that this is what he really wants and needs. I emphasize that such searching is very common at his stage of life. Once I am satisfied that he is not psychiatrically sick I reassure him of this fact and he invariably feels the burden of doubt about his sanity lifted.

The first phase of treatment is spent discussing the basic events of his life so far and the way that he has reacted to many of the experiences that he has had. I often start with a simple but very important fact—his name. Is he proud or not of his family name? Does he like the first name his parents gave him? What about the nickname that his friends call him? Even though others do not judge him on the basis of his name, it is nevertheless a factor in his own self-concept. A person's name is important and even sacred to him. To mock someone's name is to be deeply insulting.

As we continue to work together, the self-protective facade gradually dissolves and the real person, the authentic self, emerges. We discuss his parentage, his ethnic and national origin, his home background and upbringing, his family religious tradition, and his educational attainments. We review his successes and his justifiable pride and satisfaction with them. We discuss his failures and his honest admission of them. I remind him that God always gives a second chance when sin is repented, but at the same time try to help him to rescue himself from false guilt.

We progress to the second phase of treatment with discussion on a deeper level. We consider his likes and dislikes and opinions—moral, philosophical, political, and religious. We talk about his fears and worries, the things that make him apprehensive or depressed. We discuss the things that satisfy him and those that disappoint or frustrate him. We go on to a consideration of his friendships and family relationships; his reactions to new acquaintances; his activities and interests such as hobbies, games, sports, or social pursuits. By this time we are beginning to see an understandable picture of an important individual. His whole personality, temperamental type, and character structure are now beginning to make sense to him and we can move on to discussing his future plans, what he wants to do with his life, what he wants to achieve, and what are his near and more distant goals and life ambitions. I always emphasize at this point that he cannot have a direction in life if he does not have some destination in view. He must know in general terms what his objectives are and what he is hoping to achieve, before he can make any progress. He needs a basic plan which can be modified from time to time as the circumstances of the future dictate. He must be patient and content with achieving one step at a time as long as those steps are in the right general direction as he sees it progressively.

The next phase of treatment is a more thorough integration of his self-concept with his realistically attainable goals. We all have certain limitations, and it is foolish to try to achieve something beyond them. One's basic philosophy of life is inevitably involved at this stage and the patient's moral and religious principles have to be discussed. As a psychiatrist and physician my primary role is the relief of human suffering and illness. As a Christian my duty is to witness to the transforming power of the Holy Spirit in one's life, and, where appropriate, to bring it into discussion with patients. It is both bad therapy and ethically unprofessional to get involved in a religious argument with a patient, and it is even worse to proselytize him into following one's own beliefs. I do *neither*. It *is* appropriate, however, to examine the patient's religious-belief system and help him to see the extent to which it can be of help in his life. I also sometimes have to point out some of the repressive or stifling parts which are preventing him from living a full and healthy life. If the patient is a professing, believing Christian, I usually point out many of the things in his faith which can be of value to him in his daily life.

In the final phase of treatment we consider some of the anticipated outworkings of his personal philosophy in terms of his future objectives. Life, liberty, and the pursuit of happiness are considered as inalienable rights. Does he really believe that he is entitled to these? Health, wealth, and the esteem of others? Can he expect these to come automatically or only as a result of effort on his part? Just what are his expectations and his rights, and what are his responsibilities? At this point I usually ask him if he regards his life as an accident of nature or a gift from God. I generally find that if he regards his life as merely the product of a natural evolutionary process, he tends to have goals limited to personal success and prosperity, unless he has a very well developed humanitarian compassion.

If he regards life as a gift from God, however, and especially if he professes to follow the teachings of Christ, he tends to believe that he has no rights whatever, and that the good things in this life are part of the generous providence of God, for which he is deeply thankful. Furthermore, if life is a gift, it seems logical that there is a purpose in the mind of the Giver: "To know God and enjoy Him forever," as the Westminister Confession states. His duty as a Christian is to find out God's purpose for his life and to pursue it. Finding out God's will is not difficult if certain principles are followed:

1. There must be a willingness to *do* God's will when He reveals it.
2. There should be a sensitivity to the direct witness of the Holy Spirit speaking to the mind in prayer or at other times.
3. The seeker should be diligent in searching the Scriptures.
4. He should make intelligent use of common sense in evaluating circumstances, opportunities, and the advice of others.

If he is a mature Christian he knows from experience that the pursuit of God's will, though frequently frustrated by personal failures, is not an oppressive burden but a joy, and a source of satisfaction and inner contentment.

The New Testament Greek word *authentikos* means a man who does something by himself. The English word *authentic* has come to mean original or genuine, actually proceeding from its reputed source or author, not false or counterfeit. Everything I think, say, or do in some way expresses my self—either my authentic self or my counterfeit self. Dishonesty, hypocrisy, false reasoning, telling or living a lie, and having selfish motives all add to the development of the counterfeit self. Authenticity is truth. "To thine own self be true," as Polonius said to his son, Laertes, in Shakespeare's *Hamlet*. I strongly encourage my young patients to be honest with themselves no matter how painful it might be. I try to help them to recognize and admit their dishonesties, failures, limitations, and mistakes and encourage them to have faith in themselves and to develop their talents, abilities, and interests. I try to persuade them not to escape from the responsibility of making decisions and acting on them. I urge them, towards the end of treatment, to set realistic goals within the limits of their abilities and to get on with the next step even if they cannot *initially* see where it is leading. Sooner or later the destination will become clearer and they can then change direction accordingly.

The *authentic self* to me is the self yielded to the controlling and guiding power of the Holy Spirit. It is I myself trying sincerely to live according to the will of God as I believe He reveals it to me. Since I believe He created me for a purpose, this gives me a strong sense of personal identity, as I seek to discover and follow the divine plan in humility and faith. In spite of the continuing battle involved in conforming my will to His, this pursuit makes all of life meaningful and satisfying.

Self-Esteem

Feelings of good self-esteem can significantly enhance emotional development and maturity in young people. Conversely, insecurity and an inadequate self-concept are the root causes of delayed or perverted personality development. To someone with a low self-concept it is one of the most threatening and painful experiences to feel rejected. Having a good self-image and self-confidence, by contrast, leads to feelings of acceptance and belongingness. Selfishness, meaning sinful self-centeredness, is to be distinguished from self-esteem which is appropriate and necessary. The second great commandment is to love thy neighbor as thyself (*see* Mark 12:31).

To love oneself is to have an adequate self-concept and not to feel inferior. Having a healthy self-concept enables us to love others as ourselves. I cannot love my neighbor if I feel inferior, because this leads to fear and jealousy, the enemies of love. My appreciation of my own identity helps me to have self-confidence without pride. I can then give of myself in loving others because, being secure, I do not withhold myself for fear of rejection. Since God is the ultimate source of all love it is appropriate for a victim of low self-esteem to ask God to give him love for himself so that he can then love others.

The parables of the Talents and Pounds (*see* Matthew 25:14–30 and Luke 19:12–27) teach us that God has given to all people varying measures of abilities and skills. As Christians we are to use these gifts to glorify God in and through our lives. If I am a two-talent man I should use my two talents to the fullest of my ability "heartily, as to the Lord" (*see* Colossians 3:23). I should not be jealous of the five-talent man, nor set my goals at the level of the one-talent man. Part of a good sense of self-concept and belonging-ness consists of recognizing and fulfilling my responsibilities in cooperation with others working toward the furtherance of the Kingdom of God on earth. Guarding against pride, my sense of Christian identity becomes established as I see myself as an integral part of God's eternal plan. In his Letter to the Romans, Paul warned every man:

> . . . not to think of himself more highly than he ought to think; but to think soberly, according as God hath dealt to every man the measure of faith. So we, being many, are one body in Christ, and every one members one of another. Having then gifts differing according to the grace that is given to us. . . .
>
> Romans 12:3, 5, 6

I saw a young man recently who had come to the city from another state and started his first job. He came complaining of nervous tension and anxiety attacks dating back about six months, when he had been a senior in college. At that time he had developed a great apprehension that in spite of all his education he might not be able to succeed in his career. Soon after his job started he had made one or two minor errors requiring correction by his immediate superior. These experiences confirmed his fears that he was going to fail. What little self-confidence he had to start with disappeared and his feelings of self-worth dropped to a low level. He was afraid of what his parents and friends would think if they found out he was a failure, and his poor self-concept had so far discouraged him from making new friends. He felt very lonely and had no sense of belonging to any fellowship or group which could give him moral support. He was in a vicious circle. His poor opinion of himself caused anxiety which led to actual failure. This lowered even further his own self-concept, which led to more anxiety and more failure. After I had spent several sessions getting to know him, I told him that his anxiety was the result, not the cause, of his problems, and we then discussed some of the origins of his feelings of unworthiness.

He told me he had very domineering parents who had throughout his life demanded a very high performance and made him feel rejected whenever he failed to reach their unrealistic expectations. They had attempted to regulate every aspect of his development and permitted very little deviation or flexibility. They made him feel that their love for him was dependent on his pleasing them with success. Praise was rare—criticism frequent. They also over-protected him by not allowing him to make decisions for himself. This hindered his learning to assume responsibility. The resulting dependency caused him to develop a fear of handling new situations or challenges. He always felt the need to rely on others for help. Discipline for failure was often overly harsh and punishment had been too frequent and inconsistent or inappropriate. They often compared him unfavorably with siblings and school friends, not recognizing his limitations and the differences in their respective abilities. Negative correction had often consisted of humiliating scolding in front of others, and ridicule by using derogatory nicknames. I had a chance to interview his father when he was on a business trip to New York and it was apparent that my patient's parents were themselves fearful and insecure people. By their example of continued apprehension and defensiveness they gave their children the idea that the world outside their home was a threatening, hostile, and fearsome place.

The unattainable high goals set for him by his parents led to his setting abnormally low goals for himself after he had failed, in the hope that next time he would do better. His anxiety, however, caused him to believe that even these could not be achieved and his downward spiral had started before he had even left school. Though unaware of it, he was also trying to punish his parents. Failure was his only way of retaliating for their impossible pressures on him. This tendency is known as *success phobia,* a condition in which there is an unconscious need or wish to use failure to attain an unrecognized objective. He could not have understood this at the beginning of treatment, but eventually he was able to see that this was the case. He also appreciated that in the long run it would be *he* rather than his parents who would suffer the most— if some changes did not take place. Upon understanding the situation, after some initial resistance, he was gradually able to forgive his parents for the harm they had caused him. He saw that his present job was well within his capabilities, and his performance gradually improved. Small initial successes led to increased confidence. This enabled him to take on more responsibility as he developed a more accurate estimate of his abilities and resources. We mutually agreed to reduce the frequency of our meetings from weekly to monthly until eventually he had become sufficiently well established not to need supportive therapy any longer.

Maturity

The process of emotional development and maturity attainment takes a long time. Even in middle age, many men and women are still immature in some areas. Therefore, it is hard to evaluate the maturity of someone of student age. What is often diagnosed by psychiatrists as a personality disorder or an adolescent-adjustment reaction in a young person is really immaturity as measured by a comparison of his behavior with that of other people his own age.

A patient I saw recently, a sophomore in college, manifested his immaturity by *narcissism* (a condition named after Narcissus, the handsome young man in Greek mythology who fell in love with his own reflection in a pool of water). His parents had smothered him with love and generosity. He was constantly the center of attention at home, a state that he had found most pleasing. At school he was always showing off, to hold the interest of others. Lack of imposed discipline at home led to a lack of self-discipline in his personal life. He was dependent on frequent praise and verbal approval, encouragement, and congratulations of others. He had no confidence in his own worth or abilities because all his life he had relied on the reassurance of others as to the quality of his performance. He was supremely selfish, even to the point of overt antisocial behavior, and was constantly striving to gratify his wants at the expense of others.

He had come into treatment when he realized that the adult world was not accepting of his behavior. Competition was tougher than he had been prepared to handle with his own abilities. Because of poorly disciplined study habits, he was beginning to fail academically and his social life was nonexistent since he had not developed any close relationships. Unhappily, his motivation for treatment was also immature. He wanted me to help him to regain popularity so that he could continue his egocentric life-style. When I pointed out that more healthy goals in treatment would be directed towards a mature integration into responsible adult society, he failed to show up for another session.

The young child is a good example of immaturity and selfishness. He cries if he wants something and goes on crying until he gets what he wants or his attention is diverted. He has little understanding or concern for anyone but himself and has a minimal ability to postpone his gratification. To describe a child as immature and demanding is not derogatory. It is normal, indeed sometimes necessary, for him to be the way he is; but some adults are like that: selfish to the point of complete rejection of the needs and interests of others and totally unable to postpone the satisfaction of their supposedly urgent needs.

Maturity is the acquisition of all those virtues which enhance the full healthy development of the adult personality and is measured by the individual's ability to respond appropriately to the various pressures and difficulties of life. No one can achieve absolute maturity any more than one can achieve sinless perfection in this life. The two are relative rather than absolute, and to some extent, are related. It is not that the mature adult is free of sin, but rather that the sanctified Christian who has victory over sin by God's power is better able to adapt to stress and change in a mature way.

Some of the characteristics of maturity are:

1. Self-understanding of one's abilities and limitations
2. Unselfish willingness to give rather than receive
3. Ability to learn by one's mistakes and experiences
4. Formation of satisfying relationships and permanent loyalties
5. Freedom from anxiety, depression, dependency, and insecurity
6. Showing love, sympathy, understanding, generosity to others
7. Determination to change what can and should be changed
8. Serenity to accept the unchangeable, trusting God's control
9. Intelligent application of sanctified common sense
10. Self-control to postpone gratification of desires and needs when necessary
11. Willingness to take responsibility and accept calls to leadership
12. Having the grace to be humble before God and man

The test of maturity in a person is the way he responds to adversity or disappointment. The mature person will not wallow in self-pity, but will have the courage of his convictions, self-discipline, and a steadfast determination to pursue what seems to be the right course, in spite of all difficulties and setbacks.

The true Christian has both the obligation and the resources to achieve maturity. He is obliged to achieve it if he is concerned with the fulfillment of his spiritual duties. He needs to be a well-integrated person, both for the maintenance of a deep, obedient relationship with his Lord, and also for his effective witness of the Gospel to others in an enthusiastic and attractive way. His main resource consists of the changing power of the Holy Spirit which can help him to grow to maturity. This power is available through regular and systematic devotional prayer and Bible study and a moment-by-moment appropriation of it by faith.

The acquisition of the qualities of maturity requires hard work, effort, and willingness to grow. No one becomes mature by drifting through life like a leaf being carried downstream. We have to fight the upstream battle continuously, and the hardest part of the battle is combating the greatest enemy of maturity—selfishness. God wants to give us this victory, however, and we need to appropriate unto ourselves both the cleansing power of the shed blood of Christ and the power of the Holy Spirit to resist our continuing carnal nature. In this way we gradually become transformed into the image of God that He desires us to be. He promises to change us so long as we continue, in sincere repentance, to live by faith.

Evaluation of maturity in the Christian is the measure of the extent to which he is living in conformity with the will of God for him. "Prayer changes things," we often hear people say. I would prefer to say, "Prayer changes *me*." This is what the prayer of supplication should be. I tend to ask God to change *things*. He usually replies by changing *me*. I can then change what I must or He can help me to accept what cannot be changed and adapt myself accordingly. *Things* can sometimes mean circumstances, and God can and does change circumstances for my benefit, but only if I myself am willing to be changed. Sometimes these very circumstances become the means which God actually uses to effect changes in me.

Thus, Christian maturity is the experience of bringing my will into conformity with God's will for me through prayer. He either gives me what I have asked for or alters my desire into the direction that He knows is best. In this way I cannot lose as long as I continue to desire God's will. David said: "Delight thyself also in the Lord; and he shall give thee the desires of thine heart. Commit thy way unto the Lord; trust also in him; and he shall bring it to pass" (Psalms 37:4, 5).

Believing that His will is the best in the light of eternity, the mature Christian not only permits but actually *wants* his own will to be made to coincide with God's. When this can become his attitude in all things he will have attained a maturity in Christ which is his ultimate goal in this life.

8.

SOCIAL PROBLEMS OF YOUTH

Christianity is strongly identified in the minds of many young people in this country with the Establishment—conservatism, and restrictive morality. Historically, the organized church since the fourth century has been very conservative, even to the point of sometimes falling seriously behind the times. Zeal for preserving doctrinal truth and absolute moral standards, though essential for maintaining biblical principles, has often alienated youth by the way it is presented to them. Though theologically liberal churches are usually concerned with social and human problems, evangelical and fundamental Protestant and conservative Catholic churches are especially blamed for failing to adapt their teachings to modern needs. Their stress has been mainly on the vertical *I-Thou* relationship between the believer and God, with an apparent relative deemphasis of the love-thy-neighbor-as-thyself side of Christian teaching.

Many churches preach mainly the do's and don'ts of the religious life rather than the message of reconciliation. (The power source in a born-again experience can lead to a change which can significantly improve human relationships.) This deficiency has resulted in a church which appears to liberal-minded youth to be less concerned with human and social problems than it should be.

Though young people generally have moral principles consistent with their parental upbringing and background, they frequently feel that during their premarital adult years they are entitled to personal freedoms which were less socially acceptable while they were still living with their parents. They want to "do my own thing" on the basis that "how I *feel* is best." Rebellion against adult authority and rejection of the hypocrisy of their parents' double-standard life-styles are major causes of youthful expression which conflicts with society's demands.

Preaching by pastors, parents, or older Christian friends often falls on deaf ears, not so much because of a loss of principles, but because of the young person's desire to express his independence in new ways not previously available. Preeminent among these modes of expression are political activism, the use of illegal drugs, and various sexual involvements.

Once a young person has left home and parental authority he becomes vulnerable to domination by the influence of his peer group. The purpose of a good university or college is to give a liberal education—liberal in the sense of exposing the student to a wide variety of experiences and opinions. During his years in school, the student is bombarded constantly with new ideas which come from both his fellow students and his teachers. These ideas are frequently at variance with his former upbringing and moral and religious principles.

The Christian in such a situation is torn between what he has been taught and what his friends are pressuring him into. Ridicule of the established church and its supposed anachronistic doctrines by unbelieving students makes it very difficult for the Christian to maintain a firm stand. His personal faith is severely tested and to witness to those who laugh at his convictions requires great courage. Peer-group rejection for trying to hold on to minority opinions and style of life is very painful. Sometimes it can be helpful for an especially vulnerable young Christian to go to an avowedly Christian college where there is probably a higher percentage of Christians in the student body. This is no guarantee of protection from bad influence, but there will at least be the increased chance of Christian fellowship and the teaching of biblical principles by the faculty.

Campus dissent, with riots and rebellion against the administration, was widespread in the late sixties and early seventies, but subsided with the ending of the Vietnam War. The personal *internal* rebellion remains, however, and if it cannot be expressed by politically motivated activism, it will appear in another form. At the time of this writing, the latest fad is streaking, involving running naked in public places. Parents wonder with some apprehension what will be next!

Drug Problems

The use of illegal drugs continues, but their pattern of use has changed. Marijuana remains the most widespread in use, with alcohol also maintaining its perennial hold. The special problem with alcohol is that, unlike pot, it can lead to physiological addiction. It is relatively easy to give up the desire for the pleasurable feeling which alcohol gives. It is *not* easy to get rid of the craving for alcohol experienced by one whose whole chemical system has become used to its regular supply. Fortunately, however, it would appear that on most college campuses by the mid 1970s there has been a diminution of the use of such dangerous drugs as the amphetamines, barbiturates, LSD and other hallucinogens, and narcotics such as heroin and cocaine.

Why do young people take drugs? Is it for the same reason that their parents smoke and drink? Perhaps in some cases, but there are also a few reasons specific to the world of the student or other young adult. Peer-group pressure is very influential, especially in junior high and high school, but also to some extent in college. The young person with even slight feelings of insecurity finds greater acceptance in his group if he joins them at a pot party. The risk of being caught or of coming to any physical harm seems less if smoking grass is done with the group. Fear of being thought a coward by one's friends gives that extra nudge to be daring and try it "just once." The "just once" frequently leads to many times, and again group influence tends to keep the practice frequent.

Inadequate or inaccurate medical or statistical information given by friends, and exaggerated claims of their own drug experiences, can lead the unwary beginner astray. Sometimes simple curiosity is a cause of drug use. With hallucinogens, in particular, this can be a very dangerous game.

Drug use has also become a symbol of independence to the youth of today. It *is* illegal—and therefore using drugs gives a sense of belonging to the Now Generation. By flaunting this practice they are rebelling against their parents' generation and all authority figures who they feel are responsible for the world's ills. The Christian in this situation should remember the Fifth Commandment to "honour thy father and thy mother" (*see* Exodus 20:12). He should also remember that "the powers that be are ordained of God" (*see* Romans 13:1). Thus, the ultimate authority figure rebelled against is God himself.

Probably the most serious causes of drug use are those in which the objective is escape. Escape from an unhappy home in which relations between a parent and child are severely strained can sometimes be temporarily achieved by withdrawal to the child's own room for some "hash." Worse than problems at home, which the young person will be able to leave eventually anyway, are problems within oneself. To use drugs as an attempt to escape from internal problems is one of the unhappiest of illusions. Boyfriend or girl-friend problems, broken love affairs, financial problems, academic difficulties, inability to make friends, and episodes of anxiety and depression can all be temporarily escaped by using drugs—but they will never provide permanent solutions.

Arguments against the use of drugs for the Christian are equally valid for alcohol and nicotine. Some would include caffeine, a strong stimulant, and avoid coffee or tea. The principle involves a holy view of the human body, and our responsibility to take care of it. Eating too much food or taking too little physical exercise should also be considered as damaging to the body. Christians believe that the human being is the most complex and wonderful creation in the known universe, not only because of his beautiful body and superior mind but because of his spirit, with which he is able to communicate with God. Paul said to the Corinthians:

> What? know ye not that your body is the temple of the Holy Ghost which is in you, which ye have of God, and ye are not your own? For ye are bought with a price: therefore glorify God in your body, and in your spirit which are God's.
>
> 1 Corinthians 6:19, 20

The thrust of this statement is that we do not own our own bodies. As Christians we totally belong to God. He made us for a purpose and to damage the body is to damage God's property, the personal shrine of the Holy Spirit. Christ has freed us from the enslavement of sin, and asks in return that we glorify God by avoiding sin and anything harmful, and by using our bodies and minds wholeheartedly in His service.

The Christian young person who is trapped in a drug-using peer group, but who desires to maintain his standards and his commitment to the Lordship of Christ, should remember that spiritual power is available to help him. Being willing to risk rejection by his peers, he should be influenced by Paul's injunction to the Romans:

> I beseech you therefore, brethren, by the mercies of God, that ye present your bodies a living sacrifice, holy, acceptable unto God, which is your reasonable service. And be not conformed to this world: but be ye transformed by the renewing of your mind, that ye may prove what is that good, and acceptable, and perfect will of God.
>
> Romans 12:1, 2

Recently I saw a group of young people giving out tracts on a street corner. They were from a local church and several of them had on a slogan button which read: CHRIST GIVES THE BEST HIGH. The young person who has Christ in his heart does not need drugs of any sort to find himself, expand his conscious awareness, or make life more meaningful. Nor does he need them to avoid stress or run away from responsibility. A deep, personal devotional life involving a close daily walk with the Saviour fully satisfies the emotional needs which drugs have been used to deal with. Jesus Himself said, ". . . I am come that they might have life, and that they might have it more abundantly" (John 10:10).

Career Decisions

Sooner or later the college student has to make up his mind as to what his major will be. Later he has to decide whether to go to graduate school or straight into a job. Often the need for a decision comes sooner than he is prepared to make it.

My colleagues and I, working in student mental health clinics, found that career decisions seemed to come more easily to those going into law, business, economics, mathematics, languages, engineering, or the natural sciences and medicine. These students had usually made up their minds in high school about their chosen career and were now pursuing their objectives single-mindedly.

By contrast, we found greater delay in decision-making in those studying the arts or social sciences. This did not necessarily indicate that students in the humanities were less mature or emotionally stable. It usually reflected the fact that they tended to be more open-minded and searching types of personalities who were content to postpone career decisions. It also probably meant that they had different kinds of creative abilities which they found they could express more freely in the less clearly defined disciplines. Students in the sciences generally felt more secure about being able to obtain a good-paying job on graduation. Those in the humanities felt much less secure since, in many cases, even graduate degrees prepared them for little else but teaching.

We found that humanities students tended to have more liberal opinions than scientists, tending more towards the left, both politically and theologically. As psychiatrists, we had to guard against the tendency to associate their personal problems with their liberal views. Moral judgment on the part of the doctor detracts from his ability to remain objective, which is essential for a good therapeutic relationship. It is appropriate to point out, however, that as the student matures and takes on more responsibility he is likely to become more conservative in his views. Once he finds he has the responsibility of earning a regular income and raising a family, his desire for a secure job increases. He can no longer afford the luxury of impractical ideals once he has bills to pay and children to feed. Identification with the Establishment becomes more acceptable when one's family's well-being is at stake.

Several universities have made available both to their own students and also to the general public a battery of aptitude and psychological tests which can be used to help the individual discover his areas of ability. The results of these, when combined with some career counseling, can be of significant help to a young person having to make up his mind about his future. To get this type of help, call the psychology department at the nearest college campus for information.

The Christian student seeking God's best for his life should remember that guidance is forthcoming with divine wisdom whenever God's will is desired. God manifests His will in a variety of ways, the most common of which include thoughts given in the act of prayer, Bible study, advice from Christian friends, circumstances, opportunities, and the integration of known abilities and interests with desires and needs. There is also the relatively rarer specific call or conviction put directly into the mind and heart by special intervention of the influence of the Holy Spirit.

Generally no single means of guidance is used by itself. God almost always gives confirmatory evidence. (Read the story of Gideon's fleece in Judges 6:36–40.) Remember that God *never* guides in a direction contrary to the explicit teachings of Scripture: nor does He guide us in a direction for which we are not properly equipped. Our training, abilities, and desires are frequently first placed in us by God before He shows us what they are to be used for. When the time is right the doors open. Opportunity presents itself when our preparation is complete. As we act on the decisions we have been led to make, we receive the confirmatory peace within. God obligates Himself to guide us into the right path so long as our hearts remain willing to do His will.

A personal testimony is appropriate at this point. When I graduated from Cambridge University, England, with my medical degree in 1955, I would have been horrified to have been told that fifteen years later I would be living in New York City practicing psychiatry. I had recently become a Christian and had dedicated my life to medical missionary service. In fact I spent a temporary assignment of about a year on the mission field immediately after completing my required internship at the London Hospital. This was on the island of Malta off the North African coast, and while there, I felt that further surgical training was essential if I were to become a full-time missionary doctor. There followed five years of training in general and orthopedic surgery at various hospitals in the London area, at the Royal College of Surgeons, and in Baltimore at the Johns Hopkins Hospital.

While at Hopkins I gradually began to feel that, although my time thus far had not been wasted, surgery was not God's choice for me. Guidance sometimes comes gradually and so, still searching, I chose next to spend a year completely away from medicine altogether. In this way I was able to expose myself totally to God's guidance without the influence of close contact with my highly respected medical colleagues. I therefore spent a year at Fuller Theological Seminary in Pasadena, California studying the typical courses of a seminary freshman. During this time many Christian friends prayed with me for definitive guidance from God as to my future.

I felt as if, after so many years in the sciences, I was ready to transfer my energies and interests in the direction of the humanities. Since I was already a physician it seemed logical to combine my medical training and my spiritual concerns by becoming a psychiatrist, a specialty in which I could dedicate myself fully to the treatment of the whole man—body, mind, and spirit. Not knowing whether to stay in California or return to the East, I applied both to UCLA and Columbia for my psychiatric residency. UCLA rejected me; Columbia welcomed me. After completing my licensure requirements, I started my training at the New York State Psychiatric Institute, part of the Columbia-Presbyterian Medical Center, in July 1965 and entered into practice three years later. I now serve as the medical director of the Christian Counselling and Psychotherapy Center, just one block from Grand Central Station in midtown Manhattan.

No one could have predicted all this years ago, but God had His purposes in mind. Many factors have been involved in this example of God's leading—prayer, Bible study, advice, circumstances, common sense, opportunity, personal conviction—factors which are available to any young person who is willing to do the divine bidding. God is able, if *we* are willing. Our responsibility as Christians is to discover God's will and totally yield ourselves to it.

Some final suggestions for Christian students, especially those on secular campuses, who are often in need of fellowship with others of similar faith. . . . Suitable churches are often not available in the immediate neighborhood, and the young person generally prefers to be with a group of his own age and background. There are several national organizations which provide opportunities for college and nursing students to meet for Bible study, prayer, discussions, and to present a united form of witness to fellow students.

1. Inter-Varsity Christian Fellowship and Nurses Christian Fellowship, 620 North Carroll Street, Madison, Wisconsin 53703
2. Campus Crusade for Christ, Arrowhead Springs, San Bernardino, California 92404
3. Youth for Christ, Box 419, Wheaton, Illinois 60187
4. Young Life, 720 West Monument, Colorado Springs, Colorado 80904
5. Children's Sun and Surf Mission, P.O. Box 11710, Pittsburgh, Pennsylvania 15228

Youth for Christ and Young Life provide opportunities for college-age students to work with high-school students and other youth. Sun and Surf Mission conducts beach missions for children, and needs Christian young people as summer counselors. There is a constant need for volunteers, and working together in evangelistic outreach provides a source of fellowship which helps to produce spiritual maturity in the growing Christian. I strongly recommend that Christian youth become involved in this type of service, and that they also organize Bible study and prayer groups for mutual growth and outreach to others on their own secular campuses. The fun, experience, fellowship and spiritual progress they will gain will more than repay their investment of time, money, and effort.

Finally, recognizing our dependence on God and our need for direction from Him, let us remember: "For we are his workmanship, created in Christ Jesus unto good works, which God hath before ordained that we should walk in them" (Ephesians 2:10). *His workmanship, not ours.* We cannot achieve it by our own efforts, but if we cooperate He can work in us a good sense of identity, authenticity, self-esteem, and maturity and will cause us to walk in the good works He has ordained.

9

....

SEXUAL PROBLEMS OF YOUTH

The comments made in the previous chapter regarding our bodies as temples in which the Holy Spirit resides apply equally to abuse of them by immoral sex practices. The problem is more complicated, however, because using our bodies sexually is not only physically, psychologically, and emotionally healthy, but actually ordered by God: "Be fruitful, and multiply, and replenish the earth" (*see* Genesis 1:28). In the New Testament, marriage is also considered a God-ordained institution and sex within marriage encouraged: "Do not withhold sexual intercourse from one another" (1 Corinthians 7:5 MOFFATT). The essential question is what constitutes abuse. The four most common forms of sexual problems that confront Christian young people are: masturbation, petting, fornication, and homosexuality. (Adultery is considered in chapter 13.)

Masturbation is a conscious act which gives relief from the craving desire for the satisfaction of sexual appetite. This appetite is essentially healthy and natural, but in the Christian should be yielded to the controlling power of the Spirit of God. Masturbation is now known to be so common a practice that it is difficult to justify the former arguments that it is abnormal or unnatural. It is not, in itself, a sign of mental, emotional, or personality disorder. Physicians are now agreed that it is not physically harmful in any way, but it can cause shame and guilt in those who have been brought up to believe it is a sin.

In the male, nocturnal emissions at regular intervals provide the physiological release of the spermatic fluid stored in the seminal vesicles. Without masturbation, these would normally occur about every two or three weeks in a young man. However, they in no way reduce the emotional or psychological tensions associated with pent-up sexual urges.

Women and girls also have sexual urges which can be relieved by self-stimulation to the point of orgasm. According to reputable medical surveys, however, the percentage of single women who masturbate is considerably less than the 99 percent ascribed to males.

According to the strictest interpretation of the church's teaching, the good Christian would be expected to have no sexual activity of any sort from puberty until his wedding night. I submit that this is an unrealistic expectation for a healthy young person, unless he has achieved a degree of spiritual maturity considerably in advance of his years. Indeed, only a deeply devout person using all the spiritual resources available to him can successfully combat so powerful a drive as the need for sexual release. Complete abstinence *can* be achieved by a young person but such a saint is indeed very rare.

For the Christian, the problem is that it usually causes guilt feelings which adversely affect his inner peace and fellowship with Christ. He feels guilty because he believes that masturbation is a sin. The guilt comes not so much because of the act itself but rather because of the accompanying fantasy of performing sexual intercourse. The fantasied object is usually someone of the opposite sex to whom one is not married, and the sin consists of enjoying the thoughts and feelings of imagined fornication or adultery. To masturbate, therefore, is to indulge the ego with thoughts primarily focused on self-gratification rather than on the unselfish giving of pleasure to another. Fantasy is almost always a stronger stimulus to the mind than reality and, since the fantasied object is usually unattainable, achievement of satisfaction in reality becomes more difficult. Masturbation thus reduces the ability to enjoy to the very fullest that highest form of human communication, the reality of sexual intercourse within marriage.

Masturbation *per se* is not mentioned in the Bible, though Paul indicts those who "dishonour their own bodies" and who are "abusers of themselves" (*see* Romans 1:24; 1 Corinthians 6:9). The "sin of

Onan" (*see* Genesis 38:8–10), regarded by nineteenth-century preachers as this form of self-abuse, was actually not masturbation but coitus interruptus. In defiance of his duty to his deceased brother's wife to give her a child as required by levirate law (*see* Deuteronomy 25:5) Onan refused to obey by withdrawing during intercourse to prevent conception. His sin, which brought the penalty of death, was not the fruitless ejaculation, but the disobeying of the law.

In the Sermon on the Mount, Jesus said: ". . . whosoever looketh on a woman to lust after her hath committed adultery with her already in his heart" (Matthew 5:28). This further emphasizes that it is primarily the fantasied thought which is the real sin.

The young person who desires God's will in his life knows that, when he has sinned, a sincere repentance leads to total forgiveness and full restoration of fellowship with Christ. True repentance involves the sincere desire not to repeat the repented sin, and this desire to avoid the sin in the future leads to the feeling of restored peace within. This is almost impossible, however, with masturbation because the Christian knows that he is extremely unlikely never to do it again. He doubts if God can really forgive him when he knows he will probably repeat the sin a few days later. For this reason he is prevented from receiving the emotional freedom that comes with assurance of forgiveness.

In counseling a young person, my approach essentially is to point out that even though masturbation is a sin, God understands, because He made us all the way we are. From time to time the young person needs some emotional and sexual release from tension. It can be regarded as a sort of safety valve. Certainly it represents the lesser of two evils if the alternatives to masturbation were either fornication or the development of acute internal tension or neurotic anxiety. Some therapists try to tell their patients that it is normal, healthy legitimate fun—even a gift of God. The problem is that if the patient believes it is a sin, he will still feel guilty.

The Christian who wants to avoid the spiritually growth-stifling guilt to which masturbation often leads should remember two things: First, if he believes it is a sin, he should repent of it as sincerely as he can but not allow the possibility of future sin to come between him and his Lord. He should live one step at a time. Forgiveness means cleansing, which leads to fresh power in his life. Once confessed, he should fully accept the promised forgiveness in Christ and then forget the sin and move on.

Second, he should so organize his life that he is physically or intellectually occupied most of his waking day. There is nothing like boredom to stimulate wandering erotic thoughts. He should get rid of pornographic pictures and literature, and avoid movies which are made with the intention of stimulating his sexual urges. Needed rest and relaxation can be enjoyed without having an empty mind which is vulnerable to thoughts and desires unworthy of his own highest moral aspirations. It is a well-established psychological fact that when imagination and will are in conflict, imagination always wins. If imagination or fantasizing can be controlled, the will can then more easily control the actions. Positive activities and positive thinking are the greatest cornerstones of healthy living. "Casting down imaginations . . . and bringing into captivity every thought to the obedience of Christ" (2 Corinthians 10:5).

A more positive approach is to encourage the young person to reduce the craving as well as the act itself. One can almost never succeed in stopping masturbation by gritting the teeth and determining to exercise supreme acts of self-control. This usually only lasts a short while and almost inevitably ends in failure, with yet another round of remorse. The psychological term used to describe the positive reduction of craving is *sublimation* (*see* Psychological Defense Mechanisms). Sublimation, in psychoanalytic terms, means the deflection of the energies of instinctual drives to aims that are more acceptable to the ego and superego. Sexual craving can be reduced by directing energy into more socially acceptable activities.

It is well known that the track athlete, football star, or competitive swimmer generally has little difficulty controlling himself the night before the big event. There are more important things on his mind, and in any case he often believes (erroneously) that continence during the previous day or two will enhance his athletic performance later. The essential point is that substitution of athletic activities for masturbation has provided an alternative focus for emotional energies.

We are not all competitive athletes, but the same principle can be applied to any healthy activity which sufficiently engrosses the individual's interest and enthusiasm. Intellectual or social pursuits which absorb his time and energies help to take his mind off his sexual urges. Paradoxically, even dating can actually reduce the frequency of masturbation in spite of the associated physical closeness to the opposite sex. If the relationship is a reasonably platonic one, even with warm affections expressed verbally, the natural wholesome activity of spending time with the opposite sex without being sexually stimulated to the point of genital contact can itself provide healthy sublimation of the sex drive.

All that has been said so far has been with respect to the healthy normal young person, male or female, whose personal Christian life has been affected by guilt over masturbation. There are, however, cases where the practice becomes, not merely a natural physiological release mechanism, but definitely excessive and therefore pathological. To masturbate several times daily, for example, indicates serious underlying emotional problems in need of psychiatric treatment or at least personal counseling. Social maladjustment, insecurity, fear of inadequacy, feelings of frustration or rejection, fear of close interpersonal relationships, an abnormally overdeveloped sex drive, or any sexual perversion are all neurotic or personality problems which can lead to excessively frequent masturbation. This is merely a symptom, however, and the basic causes are urgently in need of professional help without which the sufferer is unlikely to improve.

Petting is any form of genital sexual activity with someone of the opposite sex, which stops short of intercourse. It is essentially mutual masturbation achieved by any means other than intravaginal ejaculation. Some would even define coitus interruptus (last-second withdrawal) as petting, rather than intercourse. The significance of this for the Christian is that his level of guilt afterwards is considerably less if he did not "go the whole way." On the same point incidentally, many a married man with a girl friend does not consider petting to be adultery, and is thereby able to live with a clear conscience about his infidelity. Under Mosaic Law anything short of adultery would not be sin: but we are now under grace, free from bondage to the Law; free to live godly lives by God's power.

With few exceptions, petting is usually a frustrating experience especially, as is frequently the case, if the genital stimulation has not culminated in orgasm. The girl is particularly vulnerable to intense emotional pain if her partner is content with only his own satisfaction. A long-term affair in which this is a regular occurrence can lead to serious pent-up tension, guilt, hostility, and resentment in the girl, which can ruin the relationship. Many girls, though not really desiring it, permit petting for fear of losing their boyfriends. They should realize that they are being used—if there seems to be little more to their relationship than sex. If all the boy wants is the use of her body for his gratification, there will be no lasting or meaningful reward for her. However painful it might be, she should discontinue her association with him as soon as possible. "As a mad man who casteth firebrands, arrows, and death, So is the man that deceiveth his neighbour, and saith, Am not I in sport?" (Proverbs 26:18, 19).

In a Christian relationship there must be a mutual agreement between the couple as to the limits beyond which they will not go. No one else should dictate what those limits should be. The lines will, in fact, be set on the basis of the extent of their guilt, their previous experience with each other or earlier sex partners, and their level of spiritual maturity and love for the Lord. Reasonable degrees of demonstration of affection between a Christian couple in love are desirable, appropriate, and necessary in the development of their relationship.

The couple sincerely desiring the Lord's will in their lives know that self-control before marriage will be rewarded with God's richest blessings later. On the other hand, failure to maintain the standard they have agreed on should not be permitted to lead to spiritual depression. Repentance and trusting the Holy Spirit for future strength and control leads to total forgiveness from God, which restores fellowship in the Lord so that their spiritual growth together can continue. (*See* chapter 10.)

Fornication is any out-of-wedlock sexual intercourse with the opposite sex. Unlike masturbation, it is expressly forbidden in the

Bible, being mentioned over thirty times in the New Testament alone.

It must be repeated that the comments that follow are intended for believing Christians who want to serve the Lord, and who therefore are conversant with and desirous of following biblical teachings. This chapter is not an attempt to defend Christian principles against the opinions of unbelievers in our society. No one is forced to be a Christian. It is a matter of free will. Those who reject the Gospel of Christ should not be judged by us according to its standards. God will deal with them with His perfect justice, love, and mercy as He sees fit.

In the providence of God, our desire towards union with the opposite sex is given to bring people together in families both for mutual comfort and companionship and also to provide a home in which to raise children. For this reason love is an essential ingredient in the mating process because it enables a commitment to each other without which no stability could be achieved. Sexual activity without love, in or out of marriage, is merely the gratification of a basic drive. Even if both participants fully desire it, such activity lacks the deeper emotional satisfaction which comes when it is the expression of mutual love, commitment, and responsibility.

Sexual activity *with* love, but out of marriage, such as between an engaged couple intending soon to get married, is a different problem. Personally, I counsel them to wait if at all possible and point out that the biblical standard remains *chastity before marriage*. An engaged couple who do not have sex can use their time together to develop many areas of interest which will strengthen their relationship in marriage. They also do not run the risk of becoming bored with sex, which frequently happens if it is the main activity of their relationship. Getting to know each other better before marriage, other than in a sexual context, will give the couple a deeper knowledge and understanding of each other. Genuine love is a total sacrifice of one's own desires for the betterment of the other. This implies giving to meet *needs* as distinct from *wants*. This can only be fully achieved within the mutual commitment and responsibility of matrimony.

Since fornication is sought mainly for the relaxation of tension and the pleasurable satisfaction of the libido, those indulging in it are not usually inclined to accept the sacrifices and responsibilities of the deeper relationship. Before the New Morality descended upon us, extramarital sex caused external anxiety and guilt. Now with this so-called enlightenment the question for both sexes, but especially for women, is no longer *if* she will perform but *how*. Her adequacy is being evaluated each time she has sex and she has a new type of internal anxiety and guilt. So much emphasis is put on technique and quality of performance that much of the spontaneity of the sex act is being lost. Also, whereas in Victorian times love was often experienced without sex, now the "enlightened ones" seek to have sex without love.

Fornication almost always involves the sin of exploitation, using the other person for sexual gratification with little desire to give in return. It is selfishly treating another human being as a plaything, which is a degradation of love. Promiscuity, or having several different sex partners, whether in series or in parallel, has an additional aftermath. A man who for some years has enjoyed the excitement and intense stimulation of many women finds it much harder to be satisfied with one after he has married. Rudyard Kipling in his poem, "The Ladies," expresses it perfectly: "I've taken my fun where I've found it; An' now I must pay for my fun, For the more you 'ave known of the others, The less you will settle to one."

Other problems in a life filled with sexual indulgence include unwanted pregnancy, venereal disease, and shame and guilt feelings leading to self-depreciation. There may also be the painful experience of a broken heart and loss of self-esteem when the relationship is terminated. This is especially the case with an engaged couple having premarital sex. The emotional scars left if the engagement is broken can remain as painful, lifelong memories.

In my opinion, the teachings of the church through the centuries have overemphasized the seriousness of extramarital sex to the point where anything to do with sex is often regarded as sinful. In the Gospels, as distinct from the Epistles, the Lord was far more condemnatory of the sins of pride and greed than He was of sexual sins. To the woman taken in the act of adultery He said, "Neither do I condemn thee: go, and sin no more" (*see* John 8:11). Sex has been the great taboo subject rarely mentioned in Christian homes, with the result that some children grow up identifying it with the work of the devil. The psychological and emotional damage done to children and adolescents by false guilt about the subject is far greater than any harm that could have resulted from an early frank sexual education. The vast majority of Christian adolescents I have seen in my office have learned the facts of life not from their parents, but from other adolescents who themselves have inadequate knowledge contaminated with inaccuracies, perversions, and immoral principles. (*See* chapter 6.)

I am especially concerned with two attitudes on the part of Christians regarding illicit sex: being judgmental and being jealous. Whether he was raised in a Christian home or was converted as an adult, the Christian tends to have strong feelings about the extramarital sex practices that he sees going on in today's society. Some of his friends may be either living with their girl friends or at least spending nights together with them. He believes that all extramarital sex is sinful and experiences feelings of condemnation towards them. He tends to think of sexual indulgence as the big sin for which God will surely bring divine punishment in the long run. His hostile feelings detract from his ability to love his friends in spite of their sin. As a Christian he should hate the sin but love the sinner, and this he finds hard to do if he sees sexual sin as worse than other sins.

The non-Christian's sin is essentially one: that of rejecting Jesus Christ as his Saviour and Lord. All other sins follow from it in the non-Christian, just as sin in the Christian is the result of temporarily turning his back on the leadership and love of Christ. As Christians we have a duty to our unsaved friends to be loving and understanding. If Christ is not their Lord, they cannot be expected to live up to His holy standards. We should not be judgmental about what they are doing with their lives. It is God's prerogative to condemn or to forgive. Our responsibility to them and to God is to pray, witness, and live pure lives before them, keeping our own eyes on Jesus and being careful that we ourselves are walking closely with Him.

Finally, the Christian young person has to contend with jealous feelings. He has as strong sex drives as his pagan friends, but his Christian commitment forbids him to enjoy them for the many years he often has to wait until marriage. During periods of spiritual depression he resents the fact that he cannot have both sexual enjoyment and inner peace with God. If he chooses to avoid premarital sexual activity he believes he will have continuing fellowship with Christ, but that he will remain vulnerable to unsatisfied sexual urges, and have periods of resentment toward God and jealousy towards others. If he indulges in sexual intercourse or even petting he knows he will have intense guilt feelings and loss of inner peace. Also, for as long as he desires to continue living the Christian life there is a limit to how much he can enjoy sinning. The Holy Spirit is a very powerful influence constantly wooing him lovingly but firmly back to the fold. We should never feel guilty about having God-created sexual drives. God is greater than these drives and can rechannel their energies. The Christian needs to trust God and to believe that He can do this in his life. Feelings of resentment and jealousy about other people's sexual activities will then become less.

In our culture I am convinced that early marriage is not the answer to the dilemma of "the Bible versus sex"! Marriage between two immature young people, not yet finished with their education or training is fraught with many more problems and difficulties than continuing the single life with all its temptations would be. I believe the answer is to deepen one's fellowship with Christ and to invoke the power of God to help control sexual craving and keep it within manageable limits. Frankly acknowledging the tensions and conflicts is much healthier and more effective than pretending they don't exist. If the Christian *does* fail, he can take comfort from the fact that God is even more willing to forgive and forget than the sinner is to confess. It is not a disaster to feel one has fallen temporarily from grace. It *is* a disaster to allow continuing uncontrolled indulgence to blunt one's spiritual sensitivity to the point where faith is lost. This will not happen if repentance is sincere. God understands and loves the sinner and desires to bring him through all life's trials and temptations to the point of spiritual maturity and sanctification.

Homosexuality—is it a crime, an illness, or a sin? This controversy has occupied legal, medical, and religious leaders for thousands of years and we are not much nearer a conclusion than were the ancient Greeks who argued about it during the millennium before Christ. The word, by the way, is not derived from the Latin word *homo* meaning "a man," but from the Greek word *homo* meaning "same." *Hetero* means "other."

First, from the legal point of view it seems that most modern societies are gradually liberalizing laws, making it no longer a crime for consenting adults of the same sex to practice mutual genital stimulation in private. In most countries it is still illegal if done overtly, if used for mercenary exploitation, or if there has been seduction of minors. With these three exceptions, most civil authorities will not usually attempt to prosecute offenders even if local laws have not yet been formally liberalized.

Second, from the medical or psychiatric point of view, homosexuality has until recently been generally regarded as a personality disorder and a sexual perversion amenable to treatment if the patient so desired.

However, in December 1973 the board of trustees of the American Psychiatric Association approved a change in their official diagnostic manual. They voted unanimously (with two abstentions) to change the category of *homosexuality* to *sexual orientation disturbance* (*homosexuality*). The new manual states that this diagnosis should only be made if the patient's "sexual interests are directed primarily toward people of the same sex *and* who are either disturbed by, in conflict with, or wish to change their actual orientation. Homosexuality *per se* is one form of sexual behavior and, like other forms of sexual behavior which are not by themselves psychiatric disorders, is not listed in this nomenclature of mental disorders." (The "other forms" include such problems as frigidity, impotence, premature ejaculation, asexuality and promiscuity.) The statement justifying the change says in part, "A significant proportion of homosexuals are apparently satisfied with their sexual orientation, show no significant signs of manifest psychopathology and are able to function as effectively as heterosexuals." The trustees further stated that the inclusion of homosexuality in their former manual was scientifically unsound and had had the effect of giving society an ideological justification for denial of civil rights to known homosexuals.

Contrary to these views was a petition to restore homosexuality to the diagnostic manual, drawn up by a minority group headed by Dr. Charles Socarides of New York and Dr. Armand Nicholi of Harvard. (The petition, for which I voted, was defeated in a referendum of the membership across the country.) While agreeing that all social injustices inflicted on homosexuals should be ended immediately, the petition affirmed the widely held view that homosexuality is an outcome of conflicts beginning in early childhood and as such is an appropriate subject for psychotherapeutic investigation. It also stated that it develops experientially and is a disorder of psychosexual development. For this reason it is scientifically fallacious to assert that individuals are disturbed *only* if they cannot adjust to homosexuality. Many of them are disturbed by the very pathology which caused the misorientation in the first place. The petition concluded with the assertion that, on the basis of clinical findings, homosexuals generally *do* suffer from multiple intrapsychic anxieties which may cause the disorder and force them to flee from opposite-sex partners. Their impairment in functioning is extreme, since they are unable to fulfill their sexual role appropriately and "in accordance with anatomy and biological reality."

We need to distinguish between a tendency toward homosexual feelings and its overt practice. Homosexuality ranges from merely feeling physically attracted to a member of the same sex to actual genital orgasm by mutual masturbation or anal intercourse. The latter is called sodomy after the ancient city of Sodom, destroyed by God for its sins (*see* Genesis 19). Lesbianism (from the Greek island of Lesbos) is the name given to homosexual practice between women, which is slightly less common. According to Kinsey's (1948) survey of over 11,000 white Americans, approximately 4 percent of males and 3 percent of females were *exclusively* homosexual, though a very much higher percentage had *some* activity with the same sex. These are known as bisexuals (AC/DC) and can be more easily treated if they are motivated to be straight. Surveys and statistics in this field must always be accepted with reservations. Homosexuals, in their desire to gain acceptance, often try to give the impression that they are more numerous than they really are.

It is important that someone should *not* be diagnosed as homosexual if his perverted act has been influenced by an absence of available women, such as that which occurs in boys' boarding schools, ships at sea, prisons, or on certain military duties. Homosexual acts can also occur under conditions of psychiatric illness by a person who is normally straight. These include manic-depressive illness, acute alcohol or drug intoxication, brain damage, mental retardation, schizophrenia, and sociopathic personality.

Most medical opinions today agree that the causes of homosexuality are to be found in the childhood influences which somehow prevented normal psychosexual development. Attempts to show an endocrine gland imbalance involving sex hormone deficiencies have had little success. Not all male homosexuals are effeminate, nor are all lesbians masculine in their behavior or appearance. Homosexuals often prefer to believe that genetic factors are involved. After all, if they were born with an inherited genetic tendency, then they cannot help their orientation and should not be stigmatized by straight society. There is, however, very little scientific evidence that this is the case.

Most psychiatrists regard the condition as acquired during early years. Freud taught that every individual is potentially bisexual at the start of life. It is normal for children and young adolescents to go through a homosexual stage of development when they prefer being with their own sex. (*See* chapter 4.) Overt homosexual experimentation among adolescent boys is so common that it is usually regarded as a normal stage on the way to eventual heterosexual adjustment. Homosexuality, according to Freud, is *arrested* psychosexual development and occurs when the adolescent fails to pass out of the homosexual stage and remains in it into adult life.

Studies of male homosexuals reveal that, in comparison with heterosexual control groups, homosexuals have significant histories of unsatisfactory relationships with their parents. Almost all have had one or more of the following factors in their backgrounds: The mother tended to be either dominating or overprotective. She did not encourage masculine attitudes or activities in her son and often openly sided with him in arguments against his father instead of remaining neutral or conciliatory. She demanded to be the center of his attention and made him the center of hers, to the exclusion of other siblings. She was overly concerned with his physical health to the point of stifling healthy outdoor activities and caused him to grow up too dependent on her for guidance and advice. He often developed an abnormal attachment to her and, by unconsciously identifying all women with her, sex with them was regarded as incestuous and therefore taboo. Conversely, a boy growing up unable to love a bad or rejecting mother develops, by negative identification, the inability to love any woman.

Generally speaking, the opposite was the case with the patients' relationships with fathers who were either cruel and unloving or weak and ineffective. They were also sometimes simply absent due to divorce or death. Often a boy did not feel accepted by a father who either favored another child or did not spend enough time with him. Sometimes the patient actually feared or hated his father or had little love or respect for him. His father was not a good masculine figure with which the growing boy could identify and desire to emulate.

Prevention of the development of homosexual tendencies must be achieved during latency and early adolescence. Mothers without a father for their boys should encourage them to become involved with such organizations as Boy Scouts, Boys' Brigade, Little League, YMCA, and the Big Brother movement. Any organization for boys with adult male leadership can at least partially substitute for an absent father. On this point fathers must remember not to be merely physically at home while emotionally absent. Some of those few hours between his arrival at home and children's bedtime should be spent with them exclusively. It is a gross abandonment of his duty to his children if he is so wrapped up in his own interests that he becomes unapproachable to them.

Third, let us consider the problem from a religious viewpoint. According to Mosaic Law homosexuality was a transgression punishable by death to both parties: "If a man also lie with mankind, as he lieth with a woman, both of them have committed an abomination: they shall surely be put to death; their blood shall be upon them"

(Leviticus 20:13). In the New Testament, homosexuality is apparently equated by the Apostle Paul with adultery and fornication (*see* 1 Corinthians 6:9, 10 and 1 Timothy 1:9, 10). His strongest indictment of it is in the first chapter of his Letter to the Romans, where he is describing the apostasy of the gentile world:

> For this cause God gave them up unto vile affections: for even their women did change the natural use into that which is against nature: And likewise also the men, leaving the natural use of the woman, burned in their lust one toward another; men with men working that which is unseemly, and receiving in themselves that recompence of their error which was meet.
>
> Romans 1:26, 27

Paul explains that the reason why homosexuality and other sins were so flagrantly committed was because of the separation between man and God. The loss of the vertical man-God relationship resulted in a deterioration in the man-man relationship. By the same token today, if a man is in a right relationship with God, he is much better able to relate in a godly way to other men.

This does not mean that becoming a Christian will automatically lead to a desire to go straight sexually. A personal relationship with God in Christ will not in itself effect a "cure." What it *can* achieve is an increased desire to do God's will fully in all aspects of one's life and this could result in a desire to change one's sexual orientation.

It is very rare to meet a truly happy homosexual. The majority suffer from a variety of concomitant neuroses sometimes directly related to their orientation. Almost all manifest some of the following problems: loneliness, depression, fearfulness, shame, guilt, feelings of inferiority and helplessness, inner conflicts, unfulfilled desires, and a craving for love which can rarely be satisfied. Unlike heterosexual relationships, truly stable homosexual relationships are extremely rare. Promiscuity is very widespread, individual commitment very uncommon. Quite apart from the specific scriptural injunctions against homosexuality, the whole biblical concept of the creation of man and woman and their incompleteness without each other teaches that homosexuality, at the very least, is abnormal, unnatural, unfulfilling, and destructive. The normal human need to love and be loved can at best be only partly met by a lover with similar, as opposed to complementary, anatomy.

Treatment attempts to correct the perversion of homosexuality are only possible and worth trying if the patient is willing. Reorientation towards heterosexuality is only possible if the patient is determined to change. No medical or psychiatric treatment can help the homosexual who wants to stay that way.

Psychiatric treatment is a slow and often painful process. A thorough understanding of the patient's relationship with both his parents is an essential foundation without which no significant progress can be made. A trusting, repecting, noncritical relationship between patient and therapist has to be developed and this can provide a model for the later development of other relationships. Generally speaking, most homosexuals have problems in relating with members of the heterosexual society, not only because they feel ostracized by them but because they usually have other personality problems preventing relaxed attitudes. The patient has to be encouraged to make a real effort to avoid homosexual contacts. If he desires to persist with any overt homosexual contacts, the goals of therapy have to be reduced to dealing only with his other personality and neurotic problems. As he begins to understand the dynamics of his homosexual orientation, he may gradually find that increased self-understanding leads to an increased desire and ability to change. As he makes real efforts to relate to all his social and professional friends in a heterosexual way, he may find that his homosexual impulses gradually begin to become less powerful.

Group therapy in a mixed group, as an adjunct to individual therapy, might help him at this stage to enjoy healthy interaction with the opposite sex. Wholesome attitudes towards the opposite sex must be encouraged. Though discussions on eventual marriage are appropriate, he should not marry until he feels confident that his homosexual leanings are sufficiently under control for him to be sure that he can achieve total sexual satisfaction with his wife. This might never happen and the therapist must be reserved in his optimism.

He needs also to practice common sense. For example: (1) He must change his habit patterns from thinking about males as sex objects. (2) He should forgive his parents and their faulty upbringing. The harbored resentment and blame is preventive of cure. (3) He should try to change his social and dating practices to females and deliberately plan to become more integrated into heterosexual society. (4) He should avoid gay bars, pornographic literature and movies, and any places, experiences, or individuals that he knows will reactivate craving for his former life-style. (5) He should control his alcohol and marijuana intake since intoxication by these leads to reduction of self-control. (6) He should appropriate God's strength to help him to resist temptation, develop a close daily walk with Jesus his Lord, and become involved in a nourishing fellowship with other Christians.

I also recommend that the Christian homosexual, sincerely desiring to change, read *Straight* by William Aaron who, after twenty years as a confirmed homosexual, successfully struggled to changed orientation, culminating in marital happiness.

A final word about Christian attitudes towards homosexuals. The straight Christian should recognize the fact that he is himself also a sinner in need of forgiveness and spiritual power. There is no place for self-righteousness. Like himself, the homosexual is a sinner whose sin is the overt homosexual act. The orientation which is a psychosexual disturbance is in need of therapy, not condemnation. The rejection, the prejudice, the hostility, and even physical abuse which the homosexual sometimes suffers at the hands of the heterosexuals are inexcusable. They are often very sensitive, talented, and intelligent people who feel acutely the pain of misunderstanding and rejection. We must remember that sometimes they cannot help their sexual orientation. Many have suffered irreversible emotional damage in childhood which only a miracle can repair. If Christians in the straight world do not accept them and make loving attempts to befriend and understand them, who else will? The love of Christ must be transmitted to them as human beings, unworthy as others, but equally in need of this love. Their loneliness and need for love is a challenge to the Christian church. We should not have a condescending pity for them, but rather love them as equals and accept them into our groups. Homosexuals need Christian love and friendships and an opportunity to live healthy lives without fear of rejection.

PART IV

Christian Marriage

10

CHOICE AND TEMPERAMENT
IN MARRIAGE

As a practicing psychiatrist, a significant proportion of my time is spent as a marriage counselor. Most of the couples I see are from Christian homes because the majority of my referral sources are evangelical pastors or other Christians. Tragically, many Christian marriages and homes are not happy, and the people involved in them are living spiritually defeated lives. Selfishness, primarily a spiritual problem, and foolishness, a psychological one, are almost always at the root of these conflicts. The most common causes of marital disharmony are: wrong choice of partner, personality conflicts, financial disagreements, poor communication, and sex. The next few chapters will examine these problems as well as preventive purposes involved in pre- and postmarital counseling.

Choice

The majority of Christian young people have been carefully taught that they should be sure that their future husband or wife is a born-again Christian. I endorse this as an absolute prerequisite for Christian marriage, but although it is the most important consideration, it is not the only one. Other factors are involved, and the fact that divorce is not limited to non-Christian couples is evidence that marrying someone simply because he or she is spiritually like-minded is insufficient grounds for matrimony. In no way can some of the Christian couples that I have seen claim that their marriages were made in heaven!

Personality and temperamental differences should be thoroughly evaluated before a young couple commit themselves to one another. If they are too immature to do this themselves, it is essential that they receive guidance from parents, their pastor, or a professional premarital counselor. At the very minimum, a young couple should talk over their plans, before they become formally engaged, with a mature Christian adult.

There are a few basic principles which a counselor should bear in mind when talking with a pair contemplating marriage.

1. He should be sure that both potential partners not only know that they are saved, but also that each is convinced that the other has Jesus as both Saviour and Lord in his life.

2. He should help them to evaluate whether both are ready for the responsibilities of marriage as manifested by the following:

Age   The younger a person is when he marries, the more his personality will change as he matures, which therefore increases the possibility that years later his wife will realize that he is not the "same person" she married, and vice versa. I generally counsel against teen-age marriages, even if pregnancy is involved.

Age difference   Acknowledging individual exceptions, I think that generally, since women tend to mature earlier than men, the ideal would be for the husband to be a few years older than the wife. A couple should be doubly cautious if the woman is considerably older than the man.

Financial   Though we believe as Christians that "God will provide" so that we will never starve, He usually chooses to provide by giving the man a job to do. Money shortage is a prime cause of argument between husband and wife. Whatever its source, enough money must be accessible to establish and maintain the essentials of a home. (*See* chapter 11.)

Education   Both from the concern of financial needs and general maturity, I generally counsel that young people from middle or upper socioeconomic levels should wait for marriage until they have finished school. Specifically, I recommend that a woman should not only first graduate from college, but also spend at least one year as an independent adult. This would make her about twenty-three years old. I recommend that a man be at least almost finished in graduate school or well established in his chosen career. He would then be about twenty-five. Marital age is close to these recommendations in Britain and Northern Europe, and I believe that this is the main reason that there is in these countries a divorce rate of less than a third of that in North America. Here, seven out of ten divorces occur in the *first three years* of marriage, clear evidence of immaturity as a major cause.

General Maturity   Sometimes a good test of readiness for marriage is the willingness of both people *not* to marry if circumstances indicate that as the best course. Postponement of gratification of wants and needs is a cardinal sign of maturity. In this context, the maturity of the couple is manifested by the fact that their decision is solidly based on rational choice. The decision to marry now, rather than later, should be volitional, not emotional. If a man says he cannot live *without* his girl, he is not ready to live *with* her.

3. The counselor should help the young couple to understand thoroughly the implications of ethnic, cultural, or socioeconomic differences. There are no scriptural injunctions against cross-racial marriages. However, a couple with different skin colors should carefully consider, in the context of their expected life-style, friendships, and social pursuits, the effects of their union on themselves and their children. Likewise, major cultural factors such as differences in primary language, family backgrounds and expectations, should be thoroughly evaluated. I especially view with caution a situation in which one partner is significantly wealthier, better educated, or more intelligent. Differences in religious background should be of little importance (assuming that both are born-again Christians) on condition that each respects the other's opinions on secondary issues.

4. The counselor should be sure that the couple believe that they really love each other with a love that can last a lifetime, despite all possible difficulties and disappointments. This is different from the being-in-love situation which is often little more than a temporary infatuation or sexual craving. Being in love is usually not truly a self-denying concern for the other, but rather a self-pleasing feeling derived from the pleasure or memory of the other. It is taking—not giving. Taking is exploitation. Giving is the essential ingredient of real love. God is the source of love and only by living close to Him can a person's love for his spouse be maintained for a lifetime.

5. He should help the couple to discover, and encourage them to develop, areas of common interest. The fact of human experience is

that love can be dimmed with time, especially if there is a lack of things mutually enjoyed to sustain the continuing pleasure of their relationship. The couple should experience as many different situations and activities as possible, and learn how each reacts to unexpected circumstances.

6. The couple should be advised to investigate their emotional and sexual compatibility, though this cannot be fully discovered until the two have married and lived together for a while. If both partners are mentally and physically healthy they can trust God as to their sexual compatibility without testing it before marriage. In any case, having a few enjoyable experiences of premarital sexual intercourse *cannot* indicate that sex within marriage will be satisfying and enduring. Since much of youthful society today accepts premarital sex as both normal and healthy, the Christian couple may tend to feel less guilty about it than their parents' generation. Christians need to be especially on guard. Guilt is not always bad. I usually urge a couple not to take the risk of becoming bored with sex by making it a part of their premarital relationship. It is better that they get to know each other emotionally, intellectually, and spiritually as thoroughly as possible before marriage. They should not allow the development of their physical relationship to run ahead of the development of their other areas of mutual interest such as intellectual compatibility, emotional intimacy, and spiritual unity in Christ. In particular, the couple should learn to pray together before marriage, asking God specifically to prepare them for each other. Sexual intercourse within marriage will then be that much more of a totally fulfilling experience. Christians can have faith that being self-controlled and obedient to biblical teachings before marriage will be rewarded later by God's richest blessings in *all* areas within marriage.

7. A counselor should recommend that the couple have a thorough medical checkup. The evaluation should include gynecological and urological examination and blood tests for count, Rh typing, and serology. They should discuss with the doctor the basic anatomy and physiology of human reproduction, birth control methods, factors which enhance or detract from good sexual adjustment, and any relevant facts from their respective families' medical and psychiatric histories which might affect themselves or their children.

8. Finally, and most important of all, a counselor should be sure that both partners are convinced that their marrying each other is God's will for their lives. If they have this mutual conviction, it will sustain them through all the doubts, difficulties, arguments, and even infidelity which can occur in their married life together.

Temperamental Differences

When two young people meet it is usually the attractive features and strengths in their personalities and temperaments which initially draw them to one another. As they get to know each other, however, weaknesses and unattractive features begin to be revealed. If this happens before marriage the couple may separate if either finds the other to be no longer as appealing as he first thought. Often however, unacceptable differences in personality structure and temperamental type do not appear until the couple is married and has lived together for a while. These differences can then lead to disappointments, conflicts, problems, and even divorce. An understanding of the variety of temperaments which men and women can have may help a couple to accept or adapt to differences between them. For Christians there is the additional resource of the power of the Holy Spirit which can help each of them to modify and even change his characteristics so as to improve harmony in the home.

For almost twenty-five centuries, men have recognized four basic temperamental types. No individual is completely of one type without having some tendency towards another. There is much overlap of characteristics, but nevertheless the one that predominates is not only descriptively helpful but can often indicate the basic way the individual will react to different circumstances, opportunities, and interpersonal relationships.

The word *temperament* is used to describe the thoughts and feelings which constitute the individual internally. These often lead to traits that unconciously may affect one's behavior. Paul calls this the "natural man" or the "old nature" in his Epistles. *Personality* is the word used to describe the external expression of temperament. It is the outward manifestation of the inner workings of the mind, emotions, and will. (*See* chapter 2.) *Character* is the totality of all distinctive features which make the individual unique—the *real you.*

Empedocles (490–430 B.C.) taught that the world consisted of four essential elements: earth—cold and dry; fire—warm and dry; air—warm and moist; and water—cold and moist. Hippocrates (460–375 B.C.) applied these principles in his description of the four humors which made up man. They are respectively: black bile, yellow bile, blood, and phlegm. He taught that human temperamental types and mental and emotional qualities could be described by the relative proportions of these humors in any one individual. We still use these descriptions today and a brief examination of their qualities can help us to understand one another better. Remember however, as you read these descriptions, that very few people completely fit one stereotype.

Melancholic   The cold dry earth of Empedocles and the black bile of Hippocrates equates to the sad, often depressed person described by the late Karl Gustav Jung, the Swiss psychiatrist, as the *introvert-thinking type.* The melancholic, like all other types, has both strengths and weaknesses. His strengths are as follows: He tends to be clever, thoughtful, and sensitive. He is a logical thinker with an analytic attention to detail. He is usually aesthetic, creative and artistic, and sets idealistically high standards. He is also humble, loyal, faithful as a friend, dependable, and even self-sacrificing. He is usually sober, reserved, and quiet.

By contrast, the melancholic's weaknesses are these: He tends to be too introspective, hypochondriacal, easily offended, and suspicious to the point of paranoia. He is pessimistic, indecisive, fearful, and afraid of failure. He may be theoretical and totally impractical. He is often in a gloomy mood, easily depressed, frequently anxious, and withdrawn from others by tending to be unsociable, rigid, critical, or negative. Extreme cases can lead to the development of schizophrenia or recurrent endogenous depressions.

Choleric   Here is the warm dry fire and the yellow bile which represent the irascible person described by Jung as the *extravert-thinking type.* The choleric's strengths are that he is optimistic, confident, ambitious, and energetic. He is strong-willed, practical, yet sometimes intuitive rather than rational. He is an aggressive, decisive leader with an independent pioneering spirit. He is industrious and self-sufficient and strives with dogged determination to finish whatever he has started even if his original premise was uncertain or even actually wrong.

His weaknesses consist of the selfish use of his good qualities. He can be cruel, ruthless, proud, inconsiderate, and lacking in compassion for others. He can also be unemotional, sarcastic, or crafty, and domineering. He is frequently hot-tempered, easily frustrated, holds grudges, and nurses thoughts of revenge. He is also impulsive, excitable, changeable, restless, impetuous, and touchy. When he's in a bad mood, stay away from him! Extreme examples of the choleric type are found in dictators, criminals, and antisocial personalities. Such was Saul of Tarsus before his dramatic Damascus Road conversion.

Sanguine   The sanguine person corresponds to the warm moist air and the humor: blood. He is Jung's *extravert-feeling* type. His strengths lie in his ability to enjoy life. He is friendly, sociable, outgoing, cheerful, talkative, lively, carefree, personable, attractive, and easygoing. Although warmly responsive to others, he is not a good listener. He is, however, compassionate and able to love, empathize with, and care for others. He is optimistic about the future, enjoys the present and enthusiastic in all that he undertakes. A good initiator, he might need a choleric friend to help him complete what he had started.

His weaknesses obviously are the results of his good points, taken to extremes. His optimism is often unrealistic, and his superficial enthusiasm wanes in the face of obstacles. He has little guts or determination and can become emotionally unstable, with angry outbursts. He tends to be impatient and restless, and under conditions of adversity he is likely to become fearful, weak-willed, undependable, undisciplined, and disorganized. He is egotistical and egocentric and these traits grow worse with age. He is easily tempted sexually and has difficulty controlling his use of drugs and alcohol. Serious maladjustments in the sanguine type could lead to manic-depressive illness, cyclothymic personality (mood swings), and various other disorders, including addictions and sexual perversions.

Phlegmatic   The cold moist water of Empedocles and the phlegm of Hippocrates correspond in the phlegmatic temperament with Jung's *introvert-feeling type.* This person is calm, easygoing, conservative, diplomatic, and humorous. He possesses a reasonable degree of practical efficiency and dependability. He can be a good listener and thoughtful advisor. He is not easily upset, can work well under pressure, and maintain high standards without the burden of perfectionism. He is reliable, thoughtful, peaceful, careful, tactful, controlled, and even-tempered.

The phlegmatic's weaknesses are that he is hard to arouse to any level of enthusiasm; he tends to be passive, apathetic, slow, lazy, indecisive, unmotivated, and has little initiative. He is usually a spectator rather than a performer, is self-protective, somewhat mean and stingy, and prone to tease or annoy others because of his own insecurity and fearfulness. The phlegmatic type, if pathologically sick, would be diagnosed as an inadequate personality, a neurasthenic, or sometimes even as a schizophrenic if reality contact has been lost.

Having described the good and bad points of the four basic temperamental types, it is instructive to compare and contrast them with each other, especially since everyone has some characteristics of at least two of them. Husbands and wives should study these differences because many conflicts in marriage can be avoided by early mutual understanding of the other's qualities. Introverts tend to be fearful—extraverts, hostile. All can be selfish, but can be changed if they are willing to let God do the changing.

The characteristics just described apply to any age, though they tend to be most noticeable at particular times in life. The sanguine happy-go-lucky type is especially seen in the hotheaded unrealistic enthusiasm of youth. The choleric person is typically a man in the prime of life who is driving to establish himself in his career. The melancholic is classically seen in late middle age. The disappointments of life have brought him to a sad withdrawal in which he can think deeply but wants no longer to be involved with the painful world outside. The phlegmatic is often most clearly revealed in the elderly person who wants to be taken care of by all available benefits and is constantly demanding attention from his spouse, family, friends, and neighbors. Remember, however, that some physically fit and mentally healthy people can remain sanguine even into old age, just as some unhappy young people can become prematurely phlegmatic.

Outgoing sanguine types are found in such professions as salesmen, actors, evangelists, lecturers, advertisers, stewardesses, and public speakers. Cholerics tend to go into the armed services, construction work, manufacturing and production, and any authoritative roles which enable them to express their leadership drives. They make good administrative assistants and personal secretaries. Melancholics tend to become physicians, lawyers, musicians, artists, inventors, and philosophers. Phlegmatics are often good diplomats, accountants, technicians, waitresses, teachers, and airline pilots. From the Scriptures we clearly see Moses as the deep and sensitive melancholic, Paul as the driving, ambitious choleric, Peter as the optimistic, enthusiastic sanguine, and Abraham as the controlled and dependable phlegmatic.

In summary, let us use a modern analogy of the saga of the automobile: The melancholic conceives and designs it; the choleric constructs and markets it; the sanguine advertises and sells it; and the phlegmatic buys and enjoys it. These are complementary uses of the strengths of the different types. The weaknesses of the types as they might apply to interpersonal relationships are best summed up by Pastor Tim LaHaye in his book *Spirit-Controlled Temperament.* He states, "The sanguine type enjoys people, and then forgets them. The melancholic is annoyed with people, but lets them go their own crooked ways. The choleric makes use of people for his own benefit; afterwards, he ignores them. The phlegmatic studies people with a supercilious indifference."

Let us now apply some examples of our understanding of temperamental differences to the special interpersonal relationships of marriage. If a married man can learn to understand both his own and his wife's basic personality and temperament traits, he will be that much better able to deal with the inevitable conflicts which can result from their differences. For example, a choleric husband with a phlegmatic wife would be driven wild with frustration by her general lack of enthusiasm. She, on the other hand, would become quickly exhausted by his demands and expectations. A deeply thoughtful melancholic husband would find his superficially happy, sanguine wife very irritating. He would see her as lacking in understanding or even concern about serious problems. She would find him dull and uninspiring, reliable when needed, but usually unexciting. If the couples involved in these two examples could more clearly understand themselves and their own partners, they would be much better able to work out some answers to their problems.

In the Christian context it is valuable to use all available knowledge and understanding of differences between husband and wife, because the couple can use both their information and also their spiritual power to help them to achieve mutually agreeable changes. I can do little to change myself by just taking thought or making a few New Year's resolutions. I *can* be changed through faith by yielding my will to the changing influence of the Spirit of God. Through prayer and personal surrender to Christ as Lord, both my desires and my whole character, personality, and temperament can be molded into conformity with God's will. "Therefore if any man be in Christ, he is a new creature: old things are passed away; behold, all things are become new" (2 Corinthians 5:17).

Let us now consider the specific changes needed if you fit into any of the general temperamental types described above. Remember that the root cause of all problems in interpersonal relationships is selfishness. Pride, greed, lust, and all other sins result from selfishness which was the Original Sin of the Garden of Eden which we have all inherited. This is manifested in all of us early in life but it has been eternally conquered by the shed blood of Christ which we can all claim.

The biblical key to change is the study of the end results of being filled with the Spirit—the fruit of the Spirit. Paul lists the characteristics in his Letter to the Galatians: "But the harvest of the Spirit is love, joy, peace, patience, kindness, goodness, fidelity, gentleness and self-control. There is no law dealing with such things as these" (Galatians 5:22, 23 NEB).

In general terms, all the strengths of the four temperamental types will be retained in an individual who becomes a Spirit-filled Christian. The differences will be that he will exercise more self-control over the expression of his strengths, and he will now use them, not for his own selfish purposes, but so that through his life and witness the cause of Christ may be furthered. He will devote his gifts and talents to doing God's will, having first, by the Spirit, brought his own will into subjection and conformity with it. The more he matures the more the Christian dies to self and the more Christ lives through him. Any strength or goodness in a Christian is not his achievement but God's grace—the fruit of the Spirit *can* change us!

The *melancholic* who has yielded himself to Christ will find himself becoming less wrapped up in selfish worrying about his own problems. The newfound joy of the Lord and peace which Christ brings will reduce his pessimism, fearfulness, depression, and anxiety. Love from God will enable him to give more of himself in loving and serving others.

The Spirit-filled *choleric* will find that he will be given love and concern for others, and his ruthless lack of compassion will be significantly reduced. Patience will calm his hot temper and impulsiveness and humility, gentleness, and goodness will gradually tame his stubborn pride.

The *sanguine* who has surrendered to Spirit control in his life will find himself no less joyful and optimistic. These qualities will now be focused on Christ and service for Him. He will find, however, that increased self-control will give him less problems with sexual temptations and emotional instability. Patience and peace will give him more ability to see things through in spite of difficulties. Fidelity or faithfulness will make him more dependable and responsible.

The Spirit-led *phlegmatic* will find that his new love, joy, and faith will arouse him to fresh visions of achievement for God. Goodness and peace will replace selfishness and fear. He will become more outgoing, enthusiastic, and industrious as he becomes less withdrawn and more motivated to serve in the army of the Lord.

Changes in temperament do not happen overnight. Often they require much soul-searching, Bible study, repentance, and willingness in prayer to let the Lord change the heart.

11

....

FINANCES AND COMMUNICATION
IN MARRIAGE

Financial Problems

Next to sexual problems, I find that money matters are the most common issues brought up by Christian couples seeking marriage counseling. I am no expert in the field of managing money—indeed my own financial situation was frequently a mess until I found a good accountant. I do, however, have a few common-sense thoughts with which I try to help newly married couples. I advise them to think through and implement in their own families some of these principles:

A Budget   Over a period of three months both husband and wife should record every penny earned and spent. At the end of that time they should sit down together and, in as generous and friendly a spirit as possible, thoroughly discuss each other's expenditures and come to a prayerful agreement as to what the total monthly family budget should be.

Split Responsibilities   *Both* husband and wife should be equally involved in money matters. Each should have his own areas of responsibility and each must stay within agreed limits. It will be easier to achieve this if they have either their own checking accounts or a joint account.

Tithes and Offerings   Christians who give a minimum of 10 percent of their incomes to the Lord's work will find that He is no man's debtor: "Bring ye all the tithes into the storehouse, that there may be meat in mine house, and prove me now herewith, saith the

Lord of hosts, if I will not open you the windows of heaven, and pour you out a blessing, that there shall not be room enough to receive it" (Malachi 3:10). The couple should be in prayer as to whether the 10 percent minimum should be calculated on the basis of gross income or take-home pay. No one else should dictate this. They should be at peace with God about their decision.

Build Savings   A young married couple should start a savings account, both as a hedge against unexpected bills and also to meet future major expenses such as buying a house and children's education. Remember that no savings bank gives interest that keeps pace with inflation; therefore as soon as a large amount has been built up it would be better to start an investment portfolio.

Full Insurance   Adequate insurance on life, car, household property, and medical needs, though sometimes costly, abundantly repays the investment—in peace of mind and when a claim is justified. I do not believe, as some do, that to buy insurance is not to trust God. God *does* take care of us, but He sometimes chooses to do so through a claims adjuster.

Working Mothers   I strongly urge that mothers do not go out to work until their youngest children are in first grade. Responsibility to preschool children must take priority over having a double income in the family, especially if this would merely necessitate the postponement of nonessentials. In the case of highly trained women such as physicians, nurses, paramedical professionals, technicians, and teachers, I recommend that if they want to keep in touch with their skills, they should try to find part-time work during their children's early years. In this situation it is preferable to have, not a succession of different baby-sitters, but one person such as a mother-in-law, live-in girl, or a reliable family friend who employs the same principles of daily routine and discipline as the parents. This principle also applies to those situations in which it is a financial necessity for the wife to supplement her husband's income, and therefore has no choice but to be out during the day.

Debts   "Owe no man any thing, but to love one another . . ." (Romans 13:8). The Christian husband's first financial responsibility is not to get himself into debt, though this is sometimes unavoidable in such justifiable circumstances as loans for education, car, furniture, and mortgage on a first home. Paying off one's debts must be given high priority because interest payments are wasted money. I have even advised some families to pay up their debts quickly, even if tithes have to be temporarily reduced, so that once they are completely out of debt they can increase and make up the amount owed to God. We are stewards of all God's gifts to us and we are responsible to Him directly for a proper use of the money we earn from the skills and talents He has bestowed upon us.

Communication

"Therefore is the name of it called Babel; because the Lord did there confound the language of all the earth" (Genesis 11:9). Communication breakdown resulted in the separation and scattering of people all over the surface of the earth into groups of like tongue. Man thence became the territorial animal which he still is today. Communication breakdown still results in separation, not only among nations but in families and between married couples.

Good communication results from a mutual understanding of meanings and feelings. For this reason it is similar to the word *communion,* the word which brings an experience of integrated historic facts, their meanings, and the feelings they engender to all participants. The purpose of communication is to be accepted and understood, but also to produce meaningful action. It can lead to *persuasion* which is action with shared meanings. Action without shared meanings is manipulation or conning.

Communication is not only verbal. The "silent treatment" can be a very effective way of getting a message across. Nonverbal communication can be very significant and meaningful—actions speak louder than words. All my speaking is empty hypocrisy if my life is not consistent with what I say.

Speech is only one part of good communication. The second part is hearing or listening. The third is understanding and responding, whether this is by agreeing or disagreeing. Many times in a conversation I have found myself thinking out what I am about to say and not listening to what is presently being said by another. He is therefore not communicating his thoughts to me because I am not listening. I am too selfishly preoccupied with my own opinion. Thus, I cannot properly understand the other's point of view and I cannot respond appropriately. I must remember not only to listen to the facts he is trying to impart to me, but also try to read the underlying meanings and the emotions which are related to those facts. Only then will I be able to respond appropriately.

Henry Kissinger's "shuttle diplomacy" in the Middle East has achieved some measure of success because by going back and forth between Tel Aviv or Jerusalem and Cairo or Damascus he has created good communication. Each trip enables him to understand thoroughly the point of view of the nation he is visiting and to explain their enemies' opinions. By patience and hard work he has achieved at least enough agreement for the Arabs and Israelis to stop killing each other and to sit down and talk and try to work out a permanent solution.

We also need some shuttle diplomacy in our homes, but it doesn't have to be stimulated by a third party. Husbands and wives should be able to work things out between themselves. The key to success is to remember that good communication consists of three parts: speaking, listening, and responding. These require patience, humility, willingness to try to understand, and above all else, unselfishness. I usually make the following recommendations to married couples seeking to improve communication with each other:

Get away alone together for at least a couple of hours each week. This does not mean going to the theatre, concert, or movies. The idea is to talk, listen, and respond to each other. A couple grow in love for each other as they spend time in getting to know each other afresh every week; for courting and dating throughout the years, continuing the joy of their first experiences together. I take my wife out to dinner every Friday or Saturday evening. She knows that on this occasion she will have an opportunity to bring up any issue that we need to discuss. This prevents any problem persisting too long without it being dealt with. The investment in the meal and the cost of the baby-sitter is abundantly repaid in harmony in the home. I also believe that it is good for a couple to spend a few days or a few weekends every year away from the children.

Priorities   The Christian's top priority is God and his relationship with Him. Next comes his wife, then his children, his job, his church, and finally his social life—in that order. I submit that this order of priorities is biblical and that any divergence can adversely affect inner peace and contentment in the Christian life. Church is low on the list in the sense of an *institution* in which a man might have duties and responsibilities. If God is his top priority on a personal level then there should be no conflicts between the others. Desiring to do God's will at all times will ensure that the Christian will be guided to make correct decisions in particular situations where priorities have to be weighed.

In-laws   "Therefore shall a man leave his father and his mother, and shall cleave unto his wife: and they shall be one flesh" (Genesis 2:24). A man and a woman must leave their parents. To *leave* is not only in a geographical sense. To cleave to one another involves a mutual commitment to separate from any conflicting influence from parents. Don't assume that in-laws are either unimportant or, at the opposite extreme—certain to be difficult to get along with. There is no point in trying to escape them by moving away as the emotional attachment remains across thousands of miles. It is better to get to know your in-laws before you get married so that you won't enter into marriage prejudiced against them.

In-laws should only step into a marital conflict if specifically requested by either spouse to do so. If not so invited they should stay strictly out and allow the couple to straighten things out themselves. If they are invited to assist in resolving a difference they must not take sides, but rather try to help their children see one another's point of view so that they can work towards an agreeable compromise. Remember that in-laws are sometimes really needed, especially when money is short. Also remember that their opinions are not always wrong.

Chain of Command   Paul said, "Husbands, love your wives, even as Christ also loved the church, and gave himself for it" (Ephesians 5:25). Peter said, ". . . husbands, dwell with them according to knowledge [with understanding], giving honour unto the wife, as unto the weaker vessel, and as being heirs together of the grace of life . . ." (1 Peter 3:7) and, "Likewise, ye wives, be in subjection to your own husbands; that, if any obey not the word, they also may without the word be won by the conversation of the wives" (1 Peter 3:1).

God has created order, and as Christ is submissive to His Father, so the Bride of Christ, made up of Christian families, is to be submissive to His will. Likewise, the husband who is called to be the spiritual head of the family must be submissive to the Lord; the wife who is called to be the bride of her husband should be submissive to him, and the children who are the fruit of the home are called upon to be obedient to their parents. When this order is disobeyed, conflict and disharmony result and lead to unhappiness in the home. Love is the characteristic that brings about submission. For the Christian, submission becomes more of a spiritual than a psychological problem. The husband is exhorted to love his wife—and she in turn is called upon to submit herself to her husband. Paul did not specifically tell the wife to love her husband, because when a woman is emotionally committed to her husband, she usually loves him.

Subjection or submission does not mean slavery, especially in these days of educated women. If a husband, under God, truly loves his wife, she will have nothing to lose by being obedient to him. She will be able to trust that the decisions of a godly husband will be the best for herself and the family. In the case where the woman appears to be more outgoing and dominant by nature, the Holy Spirit can give such love that it becomes a joy and delight for her to become more submissive. She can become more sensitive to her husband's needs and personality, thereby allowing the Holy Spirit freedom of expression through him. She can thence encourage him to mature and take leadership in every area of life. Love is like a flower and needs to blossom. The gardener can be the partner setting the right conditions for the flower to bloom, but it is the Holy Spirit who gives the life and strength for all this to take place. In a Christian home, submission should actually be mutual—both yielding to the needs of the other.

If, however, a woman's husband is not a Christian, Peter makes the point that her humility can itself be a factor in witnessing the truth of the Gospel to him and thereby can influence him towards yielding himself to Christ. Remember that Christ submitted Himself to His Bride, the church, in that ". . . he humbled himself, and became obedient unto death, even the death of the cross" (Philippians 2:8).

Identity   As a balance to the biblical concept of subjection to their husbands, it is important that wives maintain their own individualities. A wife's identity should not become totally overshadowed by, nor incorporated within, that of her husband. He is not able completely to fulfill all her needs. Only Christ can do that. Therefore, some independence in Christ as a separately responsible Christian woman must be maintained by the wife, but this need not detract from her being yielded to her husband's godly leadership.

Barriers   There are several attitudes of heart and mind which can hinder total communication.

Inadequate thinking—God gave us brains to use. Logical processes of thought must not be overwhelmed by emotional judgments. Emotions must not dominate the rational mind. (*See* chapter 2.)

Belittling, judgmental, hostile, or condescending attitudes by one partner can result in a defensive resistance by the other.

Unclear overemphasis of facts without the underlying meanings or feelings can cause the hearer not to care or to underestimate their importance. Express with feeling, but with control.

A closed mind which desires primarily to prove itself right is thereby prevented from being willing to see the other's viewpoint.

Fear of the other leads to a need to protect oneself. This leads to oversensitivity, which prevents a balanced attitude.

Prayer   It is the husband's responsibility to be the spiritual leader in the home. When conflict arises he should lead his wife and children in prayer about the problem, both privately and as a family. Verbalized prayer is itself good communication. As I speak to God I am being heard by my wife and children. I must, however, in honesty and truth really be speaking to God in my heart, not using verbalized prayer as a means of continuing my argument with them. Family prayers transacted in humility, with all desiring

God's will to be done, can break down many barriers. Selfishness, pride, and greed can be conquered when Christian couples sincerely seek God's will. Talking to God together brings a closeness by developing the spiritual dimension of their relationship. Also, through prayer a couple can often be enabled to see when they have been wrong. It can be a very humbling yet deep experience which can lead to greater respect and love for one another.

Forgive and Forget—"Be ye angry, and sin not: let not the sun go down upon your wrath" (Ephesians 4:26). It requires moral strength to admit to being wrong and to ask for forgiveness. It requires even more strength to apologize, forgive, and verbalize continuing love when you are perhaps not wrong. Remember that forgiving also means forgetting. If God can forget, so can we. ". . . For I will forgive their iniquity, and I will remember their sin no more" (Jeremiah 31:34).

Ask God for the gift of love for each other Many couples who come to see me no longer love each other. I help them understand each other better, to communicate better, and to work out some compromises for their differences. I point out, however, that the same God who gave them their first love can restore it if they both want it. They should then think of fresh, creative ways of expressing their newfound love.

Communication aims towards agreement The Prophet Amos questioned: "Can two walk together, except they be agreed?" (Amos 3:3). Paul says, "Be ye not unequally yoked together with unbelievers . . ." (2 Corinthians 6:14). This statement exhorts Christians not to marry or enter into a business or professional partnership with non-Christians. It also lays down the principle that if two people do not have enough basic moral and religious convictions in common they will never be able to agree sufficiently for their relationship to be successful. Successful communication has one major essential prerequisite for Christians. Both must sincerely want to know and to do God's will. If they desire this, God will step in and help them both toward mutual understanding, respect, and love.

12

SEXUAL PROBLEMS IN MARRIAGE

Sex is one of the most widely written-about topics. Every week something new on the subject appears. This chapter is not concerned with what can be read in the secular press. Recommendations for further study are made in the bibliography at the end of this book. I especially recommend Dr. T. H. Van De Velde's *Ideal Marriage,* as an excellent practical description of sexual techniques and problems. It is written with professional decorum, respect, and consideration for people's sensitivities and individual reservations. This chapter is primarily concerned with hang-ups that Christian couples sometimes express, and also with some of the biblical principles of human sexuality. In it I am sharing some of the answers I have given to questions I have been asked during the twenty years that I have been a physician.

There are many problems experienced by people who fail to achieve a mutually satisfying sex life in their marriage. Although some of these problems are not specifically related to one's Christian faith, they are mentioned because many young people who have maintained biblical standards of chastity before marriage are, as a result, not only inexperienced, but also ignorant of certain basic facts. Also, many Christian couples have sexual problems which, whether or not they are related to spiritual matters, cause them to seek the help of a Christian counselor.

Mutual Orgasm　　　Many couples have been disappointed to find that they were not completely successful in achieving mutual orgasm by the end of a two-week honeymoon. I point out that they should in fact be glad that they don't "know it all" so soon. Sexual experimentation between a loving couple should continue throughout life, with each new discovery adding yet another exciting facet to their total relationship. Women generally take longer to reach climax than men and therefore it takes practice, with control and patience by the husband to time his ejaculation to coincide with or immediately follow his wife's orgasm. Preparing a woman for orgasm can take a long time in marriage. The excitement of the "forbidden fruit" of premarital sexual intercourse is no longer present after the wedding. Thereafter, it becomes not only "legal" but an obligation to each other that both are expected to fulfill. Many a woman needs a whole evening in the company of her husband to prepare herself to be more than a passive partner. Verbalized affection, eye contact, and gentle physical caressing during the few hours before bedtime can significantly increase a woman's readiness and ability to achieve a climax later.

Causes of Failure to Reach Orgasm

Physical tiredness is probably the most common reason why either partner fails to reach orgasm. After a particularly exhausting day, spouses should be understanding of their partners' inability to perform, or even to want to try. Persistent rejection, due to tiredness, however, might need medical or psychiatric evaluation and treatment.

Hostility caused by an unresolved argument can prevent a partner, especially the wife, from reaching a climax. Anger, resentment, or frustration can cause tension and frigidity. Agreement, understanding, and forgiveness have to precede lovemaking for most women.

Alcohol or "down" drugs significantly affect either partner from achieving orgasm. Alcohol, though sometimes increasing desire, decreases the body's ability to perform in all areas—including sex.

Guilt, though less common, is still an inhibiting factor in some Christians. One couple I knew had been so brainwashed by their respective parents to believe that sex was wrong that they had equated intercourse with sin. They had been virgins until their wedding night and an otherwise happy honeymoon had failed to enable either of them to enjoy themselves sexually. The very thought that God was watching over them made them feel embarrassed, ashamed, and falsely guilty, instead of doubly blessed. It took several counseling sessions and several more nights with each other before the barriers came down and mutual satisfaction was eventually achieved. They finally realized that intercourse was God's gift, and represented the height of ecstasy in human experience.

Selfishness on the part of the husband who is content only with his own gratification leads to unwillingness or inability to prolong lovemaking and foreplay until both can reach climax together.

Orgasm is not essential for the wife every time the couple has intercourse. Many men I have counseled have expressed guilt because they have frequently ejaculated without their wives achieving a climax. There are two ways to view this issue:

1. If his wife is "in the mood" and is not satisfied because of his rapidity, then he needs to exercise more control, to allow her time to become aroused. The problem of premature ejaculation can sometimes be dealt with by continuing lovemaking after erection has been lost. Most healthy young men, especially in the early years of marriage, can achieve erection again in a half hour or less, by which time his wife is usually ready for him. The older and more sexually experienced a man becomes, the less problem he usually has with premature ejaculation. It can often be a serious problem, however, and professional help is sometimes indicated.

2. If his wife is not in the mood, for example, because of tiredness, she can nevertheless enjoy the closeness and the expression of love which the sex act means to her. Sexual arousal, tenderness, and intimacy can be rewarding and exciting even if built-up tension is not released. The physical contact and the verbal profession of love by the man she loves can be a very stimulating and emotionally pleasurable experience for her even if she is not orgastic as a result.

A woman needs to be reassured verbally that she is the faithful object of her husband's love. Lack of this over the years can lead to permanent frigidity. A wife should not "cheat" by pretending to be orgastic when she really is not, even if her intention is to please her mate. Such deceit creates an emotional barrier between a woman and her husband. Also his self-esteem might suffer when he finds out the truth. Occasional or even frequent absence of female orgasm is not in itself a major problem if both partners are content for this to be the norm in their marriage. Total inability to be orgastic, however, is a more serious matter in need of professional help to deal with any possible underlying physical or psychological causes.

Variety of Techniques   Every couple needs to discover each other. A woman in particular has several erotogenic zones in addition to her primary genital area. Her husband's responsibility is to find out in what ways she enjoys to be stimulated and aroused, and *her* responsibility is to teach him. This teaching should be both verbal and nonverbal. A variety of different positions and techniques should be experimented with. Ask your family physician for advice. Many illustrative manuals have been either written or edited by medical doctors. If such books are consulted it is preferable for both partners to study them together. Usually after the first few months of marriage a couple will have discovered what does and does not give them both sexual enjoyment. Experimentation within agreed limits should, however, continue in order to maintain some measure of variety and to obviate boredom. There is no reason why the sexual excitement of the honeymoon cannot be extended for a lifetime.

Oro-Genital Practices   My opinion regarding oro-genital sex is that it should only be practiced if both partners are agreeable. If it is an offensive experience to either, then I feel it is the loving Christian duty of the other to desist. This principle applies equally to anal intercourse or any other practice which either partner might consider to be perverse. If practiced, however, oral sex should be considered definitely not sinful *if* it is part of foreplay or lovemaking which has intercourse as the end objective. If oral sex becomes an end in itself, it is essentially a form of mutual masturbation. This, though not sinful when practiced by a married couple, is nevertheless a practice which does not fulfill our traditional understanding of the purpose of sex as a function of our God-created complementary anatomies.

Sex During Menstruation   Some Christian women have said to me that they believe that intercourse during menstruation is a sin, based on certain Old Testament purification laws. Actually, these laws (*see* Leviticus 12) have to do with postnatal cleansing, not with menstruation. My counsel is that it is a matter of aesthetics rather than sin. Most men and women in our society tend to prefer to avoid intercourse during the menses, though this could be a cultural phenomenon. There are no definite medical contra-indications, and it is not in any way disruptive to the cycle itself.

Pregnancy and Lactation   During the Victorian era, a man was expected to "leave his wife alone" once she had become preg-nant. There are actually a few obstetric conditions which could lead to bleeding from a placenta previa or to premature delivery if intercourse were experienced during the later months. These are relatively rare, however. If your obstetrician says all is normal, intercourse in appropriate mutually comfortable positions can be practiced right up to the onset of labor. Most doctors recommend abstention from intercourse for six weeks after delivery to allow for good healing, though this time can sometimes safely be short-ened. It is a popular fallacy that a woman cannot get pregnant while she is lactating (breast-feeding).

Contraception   Many non-Roman Catholic Christians have asked me if the use of contraceptives is sinful. I agree with all the doctrines of Catholicism which are based on Scripture, but I cannot find anything in the Bible which forbids the use of birth-control methods. In fact, I believe the contrary is the case: *not* to use con-traception can sometimes be seen as sinful if it leads to the procrea-tion of an unloved, unwanted child. Woman was made to satisfy the emotional and sexual needs of man (*see* Genesis 2:18); but she herself has needs which her husband is equally responsible to meet. Marriage has not only a procreative function. It is also given by God for our mutual companionship and for the total satisfaction of all our biological needs. Paul even said that it is better to marry than to be frustrated with burning unsatisfied passion (*see* 1 Corinthians 7:9). He also encouraged sexual expression in marriage without any thought of procreation: "Defraud ye not one the other, except it be with consent for a time . . . that Satan tempt you not for your incontinency" (1 Corinthians 7:5). Defraud means to deny that which is physiologically necessary or emotionally fulfilling.

Sexual intercourse is one of the most effective ways of continuously uniting a man and wife in the deepest sense of the "one flesh" of Genesis 2:24. It is the most intimate form of communication and transmits the message of love, commitment, security, and interdependence in a way that words could never express. In Song of Solomon, sex is a sensuous delight which is poetically described as providing normal healthy joy and fulfillment to both partners. I believe that sexual union as an expression of the God-ordained institution of marriage may rightly be enjoyed apart from the purpose of procreation. If this is true, then we are biblically justified in using contraceptive devices. (I do not, of course, condone abortion as a morally defensible method of birth control.)

Number of Children   "Is it a sin to have more than two children?" one Christian couple asked me. They were concerned with the ideal of zero population growth and felt that they, as educated Christians from a country with a role of leadership in the world today, should set an example. They had heard the arguments that the world needs more Christians, more educated and more intelligent people, and does not need more children who would die of starvation in underdeveloped countries. Since they were both very intelligent people, and could provide their children with good education, they asked my opinion about a third child. Mathematically, two children per married couple would actually cause a decline in total population, ruling out immigration, because there will always be people who do not marry or who cannot or do not wish to have children. I told them that if they both felt before God that they should have another baby, I could not see that they should feel guilty about it. Principles involved in deciding on the number of children which Christian parents should have are based on such factors as the physical, emotional, economic, spiritual, and educational needs which would have to be met for the children. The parents should also consider their own emotional and physical well-being, whether they could be good parents, and the possibility of genetically transmitted disease.

Frequency of Intercourse   When one partner desires intercourse less frequently than the other, repeated rejection can lead to hostility and resentment in the married relationship. I feel that the essential factor in frequency of sexual relations should be spontaneity. It is going to be much more mutually enjoyable if both are "turned on" without elaborate scheduling—whether it be in the middle of the day or the middle of the night. One middle-aged couple I counseled had intercourse once weekly, every Saturday night at 11 P.M. for many years. The spontaneity had completely disappeared from their sex life. It had become an obligatory routine without even any variation in method. The wife had not had an orgasm for months and the husband became distressed when he suddenly found after years of total faithfulness that he was beginning to find other women sexually desirable. After several sessions discussing ways to increase variety in their sex life, the couple gradually rediscovered each other and conquered the boredom from which they had been suffering. Couples in their teens and twenties generally have sexual relations more frequently than those in their forties and fifties. Both partners should arrange their vocational and social schedules so that neither deprives the other of a reasonably agreed frequency of opportunities to satisfy their needs. Appropriate times *not* to have intercourse may include: during menses, after the birth of a baby, when either spouse is physically ill, during a period of family mourning, or during a mutually agreeable time of prayer and fasting.

Variations in Male Sexuality   Some men have a greater capacity to love and express love sexually than others. Sexuality is an individual rather than a cultural matter. In counseling sessions, surprisingly, I find men more self-conscious about their sex lives than women. Women seem more capable of being factual, whereas men tend to be more impersonal. Men talk with each other about sex more than women, but they usually do so indirectly through stories, innuendos, and jokes. In counseling situations, they are less able than women to acknowledge their own shortcomings. One reason is that men are less capable of understanding or controlling their powerful sexual drives. A man controls his anxiety by keeping his own sexuality impersonal. For this reason he is less capable than a woman of integrating sex with love. His traditional sexual role is to conquer, his wife's to surrender. His to take, hers to give. A man's self-concept in sex is much more involved than a woman's in that his sexual success reassures him of his masculinity. Since his pride or self-esteem are threatened, he feels more sensitive and vulnerable. This is why a man is so humiliated and hurt if he is sexually rejected. On the other hand, a reasonable degree of honor, respect, and trust shown to a man by his wife will enhance his self-concept and thence his ability to show real love and also to perform sexually.

Variations in Female Sexuality   Many surveys and research questionnaires since World War II are consistent in showing that about 30 percent of American middle-class wives have rare or only occasional orgasms. This rate of failure has been found to be linked to a woman's inability to trust and totally yield herself in controlled conscious abandonment to her husband. By contrast, a woman feeling confidence and security, and knowing she can depend upon her husband, is likely to be orgastic more frequently. A woman is more capable of having this attitude toward her husband if she felt secure as a child about her father. He was the first male in her life, and her memories of experiences with him significantly affect her emotional responsiveness to all males. A loving, demonstrably affectionate, even if demanding father is always better than a permissive or distant one who might make a young girl fear that he does not care about her. A woman's secure relationship with her husband, which is like the secure happy dependency she formerly enjoyed with her father, is a much greater factor in her sexual performance than her personality structure or emotional factors such as passivity, aggressiveness, stability, guilt, or even mental health. A woman having sexual problems and who realizes that her relationship with her father was poor or nonexistent, would be wise to consider some professional counsel. Security is also more important in her achieving a climax than elaborate variations of technique, long foreplay, or frequent practice in different positions, even though these can add some excitement. Unexpected demonstrations of appreciation and spontaneous affection help a woman feel loved and feminine and put her in the mood for emotional and sexual responsiveness. Love, attention, good communication, loyalty, patience, gentleness, and reliability shown by her husband can ensure that a woman will respond sexually to her greatest potential.

Sex As a Gift   Sex is a gift from God—and also a gift that husbands and wives give each other. It is the physical expression of the total commitment to each other originally pledged on a spiritual level at the wedding ceremony. It is, however, more than the gift of physical pleasure. It is the most complete way of total giving of oneself to the other. It is the most personal, intimate, and sacramental outward expression of the inner physical and spiritual love which God has given. Sexual intercourse within Christian marriage is the highest symbolic act which our mortal bodies are capable of performing, and as such represents worship and thanksgiving to the God of love who created us.

13

INFIDELITY AND DIVORCE

Unhappily, many couples are not able successfully to implement some of the marriage-saving suggestions of the last three chapters. I urge in these cases that some ideas in this chapter be considered before a marriage is broken by divorce.

Fantasied Unfaithfulness

Some husbands and wives fantasize during intercourse that they are having sex with someone else. Sometimes this fantasy helps them to come to a climax. Some counselors and therapists condone this practice in couples with a poor sexual history, arguing that to achieve orgasm, by whatever means, is good for their sexual relationship. They say it is good for the other partner to believe that he or she has been giving pleasure and satisfaction even when the one has kept the fantasy a secret. It is argued that it is better to have a relationship that is mutually orgastic than for either partner to be dissatisfied.

I believe there are some contrary arguments both from the secular and religious viewpoints. First, as in the discussion on masturbation, I feel that sexual satisfaction based on fantasy is achieved by the unrealistic stimulus of an exciting but unattainable object. For this reason, the more a man or woman imagines a third party during intercourse, the harder it is going to be to achieve satisfaction with one's own partner. Second, such fantasizing is really avoiding the core problem, that of inability to enjoy the true meaning of intercourse with one's own partner as an expression of mutual love in marriage. Third, persistent fantasizing about another can lead to a mental preparedness for actual extramarital episodes when opportunities present themselves. Fourth, fantasizing is living a lie. It is deceiving one's loved one and introduces guilt as a silent unshared barrier in the relationship. Finally, from the biblical point of view, the practice is obviously a form of adultery, at least at the level of the mind, emotions, and will, if not in external reality.

The answer to the problem for the Christian is to ask God to give a new love for one's spouse which will enable him or her to be totally fulfilling as a sexual partner. I generally counsel a person practicing such fantasies not to confess it to the other. Such knowledge would damage the development of a deep sexual communion in marriage. It is appropriate to keep *some* secrets, at least for a while. If the problem is a burden which needs to be shared, it would be better to tell your pastor, marriage counselor, doctor, or a Christian friend of the same sex. Confession and repentance can lead to the burden of guilt being lifted. It can also lead to a deepening of God-given desire towards the partner He chose for you. Perhaps long after the problem has disappeared, confession about it to one's partner could be made, but this should only be done if the guilty partner desires that there be no secrets between them any longer, and only if sure that it will help rather than hinder their sexual and spiritual communion.

Infidelity

Infidelity is not the same as adultery. Adultery is sexual intercourse outside of marriage whether in the form of a "one-night stand" or a series of different liaisons or an ongoing affair with one other person. Infidelity is emotional estrangement and reorientation of interest towards another person and basically is to give to another what rightly belongs to one's spouse. Even if adultery is not committed, a man can be unfaithful to his wife. He can do this by relating to another woman emotionally, intellectually, or even spiritually in a manner or to a degree that he should rightfully do only to his wife.

Obviously a man has to have appropriate relationships with other women in a variety of situations—professionally, socially, or in the context of Christian fellowship. He should not, however, allow a relationship with a particular woman to develop to the point where either he or she derives more pleasure or satisfaction from it than from their own spouses. "I can't talk to my wife about it," says a man to his secretary. This can lead to his receiving understanding, warmth, and comfort from her which can result in eventual alienation of affection from his own wife. If he is already alienated from his wife, such outside liaison, though comforting, will only serve to widen the gap and decrease motivation for a reconciliation with her.

Adultery

The Seventh Commandment (*see* Exodus 20:14) was amplified by Jesus in His Sermon on the Mount: ". . . whosoever looketh on a woman to lust after her hath committed adultery with her already in his heart" (Matthew 5:28). This teaching essentially emphasizes that the real sin of adultery is the decision, rather than the act itself. It is helpful, therefore, to consider some of the thoughts and feelings that may lead to that decision. *Some may apply equally to husband or wife.*

During the first year of marriage the excitement and romance of courtship has been replaced by responsibility and need to provide. A man who had many girl friends before marriage may begin to crave the variety and ego-boosting effect of another successful chase. This lust is invariably the product of immaturity.

After the first couple of children have come, a man's wife may have gained weight, might look several years older, will be forced to devote much of her attention to the children, and may have become a less exciting sex partner, especially if she is tired all the time. The novelty of the marriage will have given place to a dull routine, and though probably not wanting to break up the home, a man might seek stimulation from another woman. This is simply caused by selfishness and lack of true love for his mate.

A man in his middle age will have become psychologically adapted to his success or failure in life. He fears that it is getting late and he might be missing out on exciting experiences, especially with

younger attractive women, which he might never be able to attain
when he is older.

Revenge is a common, though often unconscious, motivation for
adultery. A man who is either frequently nagged or sexually rejected
by his wife will often get himself involved extramaritally. Since
revenge is the motivation, this kind of adultery is almost always
discovered. The man, without realizing it consciously, often says
or does something which will give his wife the pain of knowing or
suspecting that he has been unfaithful to her.

Emotional dissatisfaction in the home, even if a couple's sex life is
fulfilling, can cause a spouse to seek the solace of another person.
A couple should constantly remind each other of their mutual love
and show it by verbal and physical affection, providing for each
other's needs, communicating rather than arguing, and by mutually
respecting and trusting one another. Any standard less than this can
lead to infidelity by either partner.

Actual sexual insufficiency is a relatively rare cause of adultery.
Most men do not seek another woman simply because they do not
get enough sex at home. Likewise, most women do not seek
extramarital adventures simply because their husbands are impotent
or sexually unsatisfying to them. A few women, however, who have
a strong need for sex, become disgruntled if their husbands are
frequently away on long business trips. Occasionally a few of these
might accept an extramarital adventure if presented with a safe
opportunity. Unless his wife is frigid or rejecting, most men will
adapt to the fact that their sexual appetites *might* be greater than
their wives'. If their total relationship outside the bedroom is otherwise pleasurable and satisfying, most husbands are usually able to
accept the discrepancy without resorting to infidelity. A woman who
loves her man and gives him all the comforts of home, understanding him, and meeting all his personal needs, has little to fear
even if she might not be the most exciting sex partner he could
have found. Being accessible and being sure her husband knows
that she loves him and wants him, will be a big preventive factor
in protecting him from the lure of another woman.

Unhappiness or failure at work—if a man's satisfaction or feeling
of self-worth in his job situation is not what it could be, he might

take it out on his wife. If he feels insecure, inferior, or low in self-esteem, he needs understanding, consolation, and encouragement from his wife. If their communication is not good, he might fear she will think less of him if he tells her the truth about his job failure. In this situation—when his self-confidence has been shaken and he cannot rely on support from his wife—he might seek comfort from another women. Achieving a successful sexual conquest of another woman might serve to elevate his sagging self-esteem.

Financial problems sometimes lead to infidelity. This can be because a man's inability to earn enough to provide for the family's needs can lower his self-esteem. Also, constant unresolved arguments as to how money should be spent can lead to emotional estrangement between the couple. Trying to keep up with the Joneses for the sake of neighborhood status can lead to financial ruin and ultimately marital ruin. A wife must realize that she and her husband are members of a team pulling together to achieve a happy marriage and home. Job and money problems should be dealt with by the wife with encouragement and helpful suggestions, not with resentment or nagging. In times of adversity a man needs from his wife all the ego-boosting support she can give him.

Criticism by a nagging wife or unappreciative or ineffective husband leads to communication breakdown, tension, sexual frigidity, feelings of rejection, emotional depression, and a cooling of reciprocal love. Lack of courtesy, trust, respect, and gratitude and taking each other for granted can cause loss of desire to perpetuate faithfulness in the home. Not all criticism need be negative. Positive correction, speaking the truth in love, can be done in such a way as not to antagonize. "My son, despise not the chastening of the Lord; neither be weary of his correction: For whom the Lord loveth he correcteth; even as a father the son in whom he delighteth" (Proverbs 3:11, 12).

Childhood hostility toward the parent of the opposite sex can sometimes lead to sexual maladjustments in later life. The boy raised by a dominating mother or the girl who grew up terrified of a cruel and demanding father will often develop fear or little regard for the opposite sex. If their childhood emotional problem does not lead to the development of homosexuality in adolescence, hostility towards the opposite sex can lead to sexual promiscuity in youth and adultery in marriage. This deep-seated cause of adultery usually needs analytic psychotherapy.

In-laws living with a young married couple can be an emotional deterrent to their establishing a good sexual relationship. Genesis 2:24 orders a man to leave his parents and cleave to his wife. Even if financial sacrifice is necessary, I always urge young couples not to live with parents, even if all seems friendly and the relationship is good. This principle, of course, does not hold for a middle-aged couple with a secure marriage who desire to give a home to a recently widowed parent. The scriptural injunction in this case is: "If any man or woman that believeth have widows, let them relieve them . . ." (1 Timothy 5:16).

Spiritual Decline   All the above reasons for adultery are but human explanations. For the Christian, adultery could be committed only if there had been first a cooling off in his relationship with Jesus Christ as Lord in his life. All explanations for a person's unfaithfulness though rational and logical, are secondary to the root cause which is a breakdown of his personal standard of morality. This, in the Christian experience, means the rejection of the controlling power of the Holy Spirit. This power, if permitted to, can keep husbands and wives faithful to each other and to God.

Handling Unfaithfulness

When a husband is sexually ineffective, unloving, unappreciative, cruel, or neurotic to the point of being a pain to live with, some wives are tempted to seek the satisfaction of a lover. Most husbands, however, feel fairly secure that this will not happen (sometimes somewhat naïvely). This is because in our culture a wife's commitment to home and children, and her need for security in her marriage makes her much less frequently tempted to stray. In fact, if a husband is faithful in supplying his wife's emotional, sexual, social, and financial needs, he will find that these go a long way towards ensuring her faithfulness. Since the ready availability of contraceptive pills there has been an increase in adultery committed by women. The feminist movement has also contributed to this.

At the present time in our society it has become increasingly acceptable for a man to be unfaithful and even to boast about it to his male friends. By the nature of his daily schedule of work away from home, it is also easier for him to pick up a playmate than for his wife to find a lover. This fact generally makes a wife feel less secure than her husband. For her to have a lover would represent a serious breakdown in the marriage relationship. The same is true for the husband, but he may tell himself that if he is discreet, his infidelity need not affect his family's happiness and security. He feels that if he keeps it a secret, his wife and children won't get hurt and he'll still have a happy home.

If a woman has any suspicion of her husband's infidelity, rather than confronting him immediately, she should take a good look at herself and their relationship. If problems at home can be straightened out, the erring man might be won back without the need for confrontation:

She should be supportive of him when things go wrong. Strengthening his self-esteem in times of disappointment will enable him to love himself and thereby love her as himself.

All known problems should be faced honestly without harbored resentments. It is better to bring things out into the open, to talk about differences frankly and clear the air of all minor irritations before they become major ones.

A wife should strive to maintain herself as attractive as possible, but not only physically. She should also develop interests of her own apart from her husband so that when he comes home she will have other than household problems to talk about. Intellectual attractiveness can be important.

She should make her husband her top priority and primary emotional object. She should avoid nagging and demanding.

A Christian woman will pray to be given wisdom for every situation and the ability to do what is best for her marriage.

Arguments Against Infidelity

The person who cheats secretly on his spouse, thinking it will be okay so long as the partner doesn't find out, should remember some of these opposing views:

Infidelity is stealing.   It is robbing the marital partner of what is rightfully his or hers and giving it to another. Affection, energy, time, and money spent on another liaison is depriving a spouse of what is rightly due.

Secrecy is a betrayal of trust.   It therefore increases the separation between a man and wife. One knows something not shared with the other and is living a lie, pretending something which is not true.

Suspicion causes pain.   Before long, a husband or wife usually gets some evidence of a spouse's errancy. Not knowing for sure, and hating the risk of confrontation (right or wrong in the suspicion, this could cause an ugly scene), the suspicious one has to live with the pain and doubt of not knowing.

Adultery is a form of escape.   Seeking comfort in the arms of another is running away from the real issue, that of facing the problems at home. It is a temporary camouflage which permits the real malady to grow worse.

Adultery frequently results from fear.   A man is sometimes afraid to communicate to his wife that she does not satisfy him sexually. He is afraid of her reaction—possibly criticism, resentment, or cooling of her love for him. He may be ashamed or embarrassed to admit that his need is not satisfied. This is especially a problem in a man with a rigid background. Note that it may be the *wife* who cannot communicate *her* lack of satisfaction.

Adultery is self-destructive.   The unfaithful partner is deceiving himself by believing that sinning secretly protects and safeguards the marriage and home. Self-deceit makes the sinner his own worst enemy and can lead to anxiety, depression, low self-concept, and psychosomatic illness. Illicit thoughts and desires are painful and binding. "But whoso committeth adultery with a woman lacketh understanding: he that doeth it destroyeth his soul" (Proverbs 6:32).

Guilt and fear catch up with an adulterer (or adulteress).   His conscience gnaws at him and he is always afraid of being exposed, with the possible result of a broken home and public shame. ". . . ye have sinned against the Lord: and be sure your sin will find you out" (Numbers 32:23).

Telling or living a lie leads to more lies. Once you tell a lie you have to tell another to cover it up. The major problem with lying is to remember what you said. The truth is easily remembered. Adultery leads to living a confused life of lies and deceit before someone who trusts you. This results in a double-bind situation. The lies have the boomerang effect of taking you further from the one you should be close to. The truth at this point could lead to complete breakdown in the marriage. Either way you lose.

The Way Back From Unfaithfulness

Here are ten steps I recommend for anyone who has sinned through unfaithfulness, but is now willing to put things right:

1. Stop rationalizing that secrecy and lying is protecting your marriage and family.
2. Admit self-deceit and face up to its destructive consequences.
3. Be honest with yourself and acknowledge your conflicts and needs.
4. Recognize that faithfulness and love are inseparable.
5. Seek to improve communication with your spouse and be humble enough to admit shortcomings, failures, and fears.
6. Share your concern with your pastor, counselor, or trusted friend.
7. Confess your sin to God, trust His forgiveness, and appropriate His strength to give power to do that which is right in the future.
8. True repentance includes confessing your sin to your extramarital partner and agreeing to discontinue the relationship. Such repentance could be an act of witness.
9. Ask God to give you renewed love and faithfulness towards your spouse—and trust Him to do so.
10. Remain faithful thereafter to your spouse, trusting God to give you the ability to maintain it. Share the truth about your infidelity only if you are certain that scars are fully healed, that there is no foreseeable likelihood of a repetition, and if you believe that your spiritual relationship together is such that confession and forgiveness will deepen rather than harm it.

Divorce

The problem of divorce must be faced by Christians from both the doctrinal and reality-situation viewpoints. Jesus said in Matthew 19:8 that Moses had allowed divorce "because of the hardness of your hearts" as a regulation of an existing practice. The passage giving this law states in part: "When a man hath taken a wife, and married her, and it come to pass that she find no favour in his eyes, because he hath found some uncleanness in her: then let him write her a bill of divorcement, and give it in her hand, and send her out of his house. And when she is departed out of his house, she may go and be another man's wife" (Deuteronomy 24:1, 2). Interpretations of this law immediately before the time of Christ were variable. The great rabbinic teacher, Hillel, defined *uncleanness* as anything displeasing to the husband. The school of Shammai interpreted it as meaning only unfaithfulness. Neither of these teachers condoned divorce. They merely accepted it as a fact of human experience, and attempted to place controls upon its use.

Jesus continued: "And I say unto you, Whosoever shall put away his wife, except it be for fornication, and shall marry another, committeth adultery: and whoso marrieth her which is put away doth commit adultery" (Matthew 19:9). Nothing is said about a woman divorcing her husband for any infidelity on *his* part. This is because under Jewish law in the time of Christ, a woman could not divorce her husband. She could only take him to court and the court could make him divorce her. Under Roman and Greek law a woman had equal rights with regard to divorce action. Most Roman Catholic and Protestant churches today interpret all Scriptures regarding divorce and remarriage as being equally valid for both men and women. Fornication in this Scripture is generally regarded as meaning adultery *during* marriage, as far as divorce is concerned. Most churches do not recognize divorce on the grounds of the later discovery or admission of premarital sexual intercourse. Adultery was the only grounds for divorce as far as Moses and Christ were concerned.

There is, however, one other situation acceptable by most

churches—the so-called Pauline Privilege. Paul, first repeating the teaching of Christ, continues under the guidance of the Holy Spirit discussing a new situation not existing at the time Jesus was teaching. He says that in the case where a married man becomes a believing Christian, he should not divorce his wife if she remains a pagan but wants to continue the marriage. To a believing wife likewise, Paul says of her husband, "If he be pleased to dwell with her, let her not leave him. . . . But if the unbelieving depart, let him depart. A brother or a sister is not under bondage in such cases: but God hath called us to peace" (*see* 1 Corinthians 7:13, 15). This biblical teaching allows divorce in the case where the pagan partner chooses to leave the believer. The believer, I feel, is then justified in obtaining a divorce and remarrying someone who is a believer. Some churches teach that the example of the Prophet Hosea should dictate this situation. This would demand that the believer wait in loneliness for the unbeliever to return, only accepting divorce if filed by the unbeliever. I consider this to be a cruel and unreasonable restriction on an innocent person's freedom. Sometimes this teaching is interpreted today as including justification for divorce between a Christian couple when one partner subsequently denies the faith that they shared when they first married. This is a spiritual problem necessitating Christian marriage counseling to help the couple evaluate whether or not divorce is scripturally justified. Some Christians interpret this form of divorce as not justifying remarriage. Personally, I do not think that Paul meant that the Christian is simply free to be deserted. I feel that implicit in his statement is the right for such to remarry. Also, in the case of converts and repentant members, a church generally has to accept a situation as it is. A previously divorced convert, for example, who has remarried cannot return to his previous partner, and his second marriage therefore cannot be regarded as adulterous, whether or not his second wife is a Christian.

A few thoughts from the reality viewpoint are relevant apart from any doctrinal positions. Reverend James G. Emerson, Jr. wrote a book worth reading on this subject—*Divorce, the Church, and. Remarriage*. He distinguishes between divorce as an official recognition that a marriage is already dead, or as being a means of killing a potentially viable one. For example, if a couple is living apart and either one or both of them have no intention of their ever getting together again, the marriage is dead, and divorce simply recognizes officially the already existent state. On the other hand, when a couple is not getting along very well for whatever reasons, thoughts or threats of divorce might prematurely kill a relationship which could possibly survive if given a chance. Too-easy divorce, now available in many states, allows a couple to split long before they have given their marriage a fair go. In Christendom until this century, adultery was the only legally acceptable cause for divorce. Then came desertion and cruelty. Now we have *marital breakdown, incompatibility,* and *no-fault* in such states as Florida and California. In one state a couple without children can simply send a notarized affidavit to a court and obtain a decree by return mail.

The rights of children should never be forgotten. They often suffer more than their divorcing parents. They are entitled to the freedom to grow up to become mature persons by living in an environment which will enhance emotional stability in their developing personalities. When a couple have made a mess of their own lives, they no longer deserve to put their own happiness first. Their primary consideration should be the future lives of their children and they must decide to do that which is best for them rather than for themselves.

Divorce should be regarded by a Christian counselor as an absolute last resort to be used only if the marriage is definitely dead. At the Christian Counselling and Psychotherapy Center in New York City, where I am the medical director, we have a policy of never recommending divorce if there is even a minute chance that a couple can be reconciled through counseling. I have had the joy of seeing seemingly hopeless cases respond to the couples' facing up to their emotional and personal problems and communication breakdowns. It is very satisfying both professionally and spiritually to have been a part of a rescue operation which has helped to save a marriage.

One final thought from the Christian viewpoint regarding divorce. We have to balance Scripture with Scripture. Whereas divorce leading to remarriage is considered to be adultery in the New Testament, there is also the teaching that a person's primary responsibility is to love and serve God. If a bad marriage can definitely be shown to be restricting the carrying out of this responsibility, it could be argued that divorce would be the lesser of two evils. If a Christian person before God can clearly see that his or her ability and freedom to live for Christ would be enhanced by a separation or divorce, this could possibly be a justified cause for it. Such an individual, however, carries for his lifetime the burden of responsibility to show continuously that such a decision was correct. This is not an easy choice, and the use of this argument (when it is not true) to rationalize a wrong decision will inevitably be punished by a guilty conscience and possibly other indirect undesirable aftereffects. Reconciliation with one's spouse remains the first objective—and divorce should be considered only when all else has truly failed.

PART V

Declining Years

14

....

AGING AND DYING

Aging

In our youth-oriented society, the problem of aging is often given
low priority. People in their youth and middle age tend to shun
attention for the elderly. This is partly because they think they
have little to gain by giving such attention, partly because of a fear
of failing in conversation or ability to relate (the generation gap),
and also because there is often an unconscious distaste for the inevitable fact that they themselves will one day be in the same
situation.

About twenty million people in this country, almost 10 percent
of the population, are over sixty-five years old. Each sixty-five-year-
old has an average life expectancy of another fifteen years. This percentage is increasing annually, not so much because people are living longer, which they are, but because modern health care is
enabling more people who might have died younger to reach retirement and old age. There is of course a male-female difference. At
sixty-five there are seven women to every five men, and at that time
most women can expect another fifteen to twenty years of life and
men another ten to fifteen. By age seventy-five there are almost
nine women to every five men.

The process of aging begins at birth. The peak of learning new
ideas and of retentive ability is during the mid-teens. The peak of
physical ability, as measured by athletic competition, is about
twenty-five in men, somewhat younger in women. From the mid-
twenties onwards, physiological tests prove an annual deterioration

in almost all major muscular activities. There are many reasons why the body ages. One theory indicts cosmic rays from the sun which over a lifetime progressively cause degeneration in all cellular functions. Obviously genetics or one's hereditary background is a factor causing minor individual differences. One preventable cause is malnutrition, from which almost all old people living alone suffer. The facts are that structural changes take place which lead to functional decline.

Loss of muscle tissue leads to loss of weight and strength; softening of bones increases likelihood of fractures; diminished hormonal activity reduces a variety of metabolic functions and sexual energy; and shriveling of the skin and collagen tissues leads to loss of elasticity and general body shrinkage. Slowed-down functioning of the white blood cells reduces resistance to infection. Atrophy of taste buds, smell receptors, middle and inner ear structures, and failing visual acuity all contribute to reducing the old person's ability to remain in contact with the sensations of the world around him. Progressively reduced cerebral blood circulation, in spite of compensatory rise in blood pressure, adds to general loss in central-nervous-system functioning.

The most important loss, however, is the inexorable disappearance of brain cells which cannot regenerate. The most highly developed part of the brain, the cerebral cortex, is the most vulnerable and the postmortem weight of a brain is as much as 15 percent less at age seventy-five than a brain of a twenty-five-year-old. It is the loss of these cells which causes the classical signs of senility. These signs are: memory loss (especially for recent events), confusion of thought, poor concentration, slowed-down thinking, apathy, reduction of alertness and reflex responses, reduced ability to accept new ideas—with resultant conservatism in action and outlook, and ultimately the tendency to become self-centered and protective in the shrunken world of narrowed interests. The rate of loss of cerebral cells can be lessened by reducing the intake of alcohol, nicotine, and certain other toxic substances.

These degenerative processes lead inevitably to emotional and psychological problems. Preeminent among these are depression, irritability, anxiety, paranoia, and somatic delusions about bodily dysfunctions. These in turn lead to social problems such as withdrawal, isolation, lack of motivation, prideful independence, or its opposite, demanding dependency. The suicide rate increases, reaching a maximum in white males in their eighties.

One preventable problem is that society tends to define a person as old on the basis of chronological age rather than functioning efficiency. An elderly person frequently tends to behave as expected by the attitude that, "You can't teach an old dog new tricks." This is a lie and old people must be encouraged to realize that it is a lie. Old dogs *can* learn new tricks. Also the old can sometimes teach *young* dogs new tricks. They have a wealth of knowledge, wisdom, and experience that the young need as a guiding and controlling influence on their energy and zeal.

The most important thing an old person needs is an ongoing relationship with one or more people who have significance to him. The International Ladies Garment Workers Union has thirty thousand retirees who are visited regularly in their homes across the country. These people, as a result, tend to stay in their own homes and communities, have good nutritional standards, stay in good physical condition, get good preventive and early therapeutic medical attention. They end up in a terminal nursing home significantly *less* frequently than would be usual for their age group.

The maintenance of relationships is the key factor, not only in advanced age, but also in the still-active early retirement years. Men and women forced by company policy to retire at sixty-five should have spent several years planning and working towards their later objectives during the decade or two prior to retirement. Continuing to work in a part-time capacity is possible for some. Volunteer work is readily available to almost all. Christian retirees should remember that there are a great number of churches and a variety of struggling Christian organizations which could provide interesting and important work for volunteers. This could be either part-time or full-time, but either way it would be an ideal form of fulfilling service for elderly Christians who desire to use their retirement years for the furtherance of God's Kingdom on earth. Such people would not only have the satisfaction of continuing in the Lord's service by the work they do, but they would also have the daily blessing of fellowship with others whose faith and ideals are similar to their own. Nicodemus asked, "How can a man be born when he is old?" Jesus answered about his need for a spiritual rebirth (*see* John 3:4–7). An already-reborn Christian retiree can experience another form of rebirth, that which leads him into a new decade or more of purposeful living for God.

I have a few specific suggestions for retirees:

1. Plan your retirement *to* some activity, not *from* your job. Think and prepare positively in advance for keeping yourself busy after retirement.

2. Arrange your finances so that you will be able to meet your needs and obligations and still live within your budget.

3. Wean yourself quickly from your old job. Keep a few old friends but don't allow yourself to keep wishing you were still at work. Look ahead, not back.

4. Get yourself either a part-time or volunteer job, depending on local needs and opportunities.

5. Consider your living situation. Do you need as big a house now? Would you rather move closer to relatives or to a warmer climate?

6. Every six months have a thorough physical checkup. The early discovery and treatment of potentially dangerous medical problems can add years to your life.

7. Remain active socially. Join Golden Age or Senior Citizens organizations. Subscribe to *Modern Maturity,* the journal of the American Association of Retired Persons, 215 Long Beach Blvd., Long Beach, California 90801.

8. Remain active at home, too. Develop new or rediscover old hobbies. Get started on those good books you have always wanted to read. My much-loved father, a retired physician, is spending his senior years absorbing a whole library of the best literature which he has accumulated during his lifetime.

9. Keep physically fit. Take as much exercise as your doctor authorizes. Get plenty of fresh air, good food, and enough sleep.

10. Continue to cultivate your spiritual life. Continue to have your regular few minutes of devotional prayer and Bible reading. "My son, forget not my law; but let thine heart keep my command-

ments; For length of days, and long life, and peace, shall they add
to thee" (Proverbs 3:1, 2).
11. Get involved in a strong body of believers. Many evangelical
churches have active groups for retired men and women, which
provide not only enjoyable activities but also warm Christian
fellowship.
12. Shut-ins should not be reserved about asking that their pastor
and other Christian friends come to visit them frequently and
regularly.

You are never old when you have something or someone to live
for. Work that satisfies is not *work* but satisfaction. What you do to
serve others' interests also serves your own. Forcing yourself to learn
and do new things will give added incentive and purpose to your
new life. Even though lost brain cells never grow again, there are
still billions of them left and keeping them working constantly will
enable them to keep on working longer. My own mother, after retirement from thirty-five years in practice as a physician, ran a farm
for several years, and now, at over seventy years of age, is taking
graduate courses in physics and biology. I propose to remain similarly active both physically and intellectually when I reach her age.

If at all possible, an elderly person should be allowed to stay at
home. A terminal nursing home is a very impersonal place where
individual privacy is almost nonexistent. An elderly couple, in particular, should at the very minimum have the dignity of their own
bedroom. It is both common and healthy for sexual interest and
some measure of potency to be maintained even into the eighties
and nineties in both men and women. Even if they are no longer
capable of orgasm, an elderly couple can derive much pleasure and
comfort from sleeping together and this should never be denied
them by consigning them to custodial care simply for the con-
venience of the junior generation. Young people often find that the
thought of sexual activity in old people is distasteful. By contrast,
studies have shown that sex not only can continue into late age, but
also that some couples have actually experienced increased activity
after retirement; many women, it was found, become orgastic for
the first time in their sixties.

Eventually the time will come when, with great age, a person can no longer continue the interesting pursuits of the early retirement years. At this point his family, personal physician, and friends have special responsibilities, especially if the patient becomes a shut-in. "I was sick and ye visited me" (*see* Matthew 25:36). This saying of Jesus compels us to a personal ministry of visitation of the sick and infirm. As visitors, our task is to help mobilize the life-force and arouse the will to live within the sick one. Elderly people especially enjoy visits from their grandchildren. The carefree joy of youth is good therapy for one sinking into despair and hopelessness. We need to be good listeners, patient to hear even that which is repeated several times. The obligation to help someone to live "in the truth" is important to the Christian but this has to be balanced by the factor of the shut-in's measure of contact with reality.

Our visits should be brief if he is tired, longer if he is anxious to communicate. We should keep away from negative subjects such as illness or the death of others. At all times we should be cheerful and optimistic, always mentioning something, however trivial, that the shut-in has to look forward to. If possible, the occasion can be not only social but spiritual. "Is any sick among you? let him call for the elders of the church; and let them pray over him, anointing him with oil in the name of the Lord: And the prayer of faith shall save the sick, and the Lord shall raise him up; and if he have committed sins, they shall be forgiven him" (James 5:14, 15). The verbalizing of a brief prayer can be very therapeutic. In this we can invoke God's help to relieve discomfort and pain, to direct doctors and nurses caring for him, to bring healing if it be His will, to watch over the needs of loved ones, and to draw closer to the patient with strengthening assurance and love. The reading of short passages of Scripture can bring added peace. Especially remember the beautiful promise in Isaiah: "And even to your old age I am he; and even to hoar hairs will I carry you: I have made, and I will bear; even I will carry, and will deliver you" (Isaiah 46:4).

Dying

"To every thing there is a season, and a time to every purpose under the heaven: A time to be born, and a time to die . . ." (Ecclesiastes 3:1, 2). When death becomes inevitable and imminent, family and friends have special prayer obligations for the patient and his loved ones, and should work cooperatively with the doctors and nursing staff.

Christians generally believe that euthanasia or mercy killing is contrary to biblical teaching. "Neither will I administer a poison to anybody when asked to do so, nor will I suggest such a course," Hippocrates states in part of his oath. "Thou shalt not kill" (Exodus 20:13). The Sixth Commandment leaves no loopholes for any extenuating circumstances, but the modern philosophy of many has added, "But needst not strive, officiously to keep alive." The valid reason for this is that only in this generation have we achieved the ability to prolong life physiologically without regard to the patient's ability to retain conscious awareness. Death is now no longer defined as cessation of heartbeat. It is "cerebral death" which is evaluated because this incorporates the concept of the *quality* of residual life. Physicians are increasingly educating the public that the terminal "human vegetable" is not *living,* in the sense of any meaningful future life. To *allow to die* is not the same as to *kill.*

Many doctors respect families' wishes with regard to the extent of measures to be used to keep dying patients alive. When death is no longer avoidable, many physicians prefer to let their patients die peacefully with dignity, and without heroic attempts to keep them alive by artificial means for a few extra days. The physician's primary concern at this time is the relief of suffering, not the prolongation of life. This is especially the case if such prolongation would necessitate treatment methods that could either bring further discomfort to the patient, or not improve the condition but merely slow down the terminal deterioration process. *Primum non nocere* (first of all, do no harm) has been the first principle of medical ethics since Hippocrates. The great English physician, Sir Robert Hutchinson, wrote, ". . . from making the cure of the disease more grievous than the endurance of the same, good Lord deliver us." The inventor of antiseptic surgery, Lord Lister, said that physicians' obligations to their patients were "to cure sometimes, to relieve often, to comfort always."

When illness is definitely terminal, it is usually better, if at all practically possible, for the patient to leave the hospital and go home to die. It is infinitely more preferable for a person's last hours to be spent in his familiar home environment surrounded by family and close friends. The alternative is the unfamiliar hospital with nurses, doctors, and assistants obsessively pursuing their routine duties. For the rich, this is a lonely private room—for the not-so-rich, a noisy public ward. Either way it is both less convenient and more expensive for the family. Another consideration for death to come at home is that children of all ages can be taught about the facts of death, and experience its reality in the context of the family. Children under seven tend to understand death as a temporary, not a permanent departure. It also tends to prevent a child growing up believing that a hospital is primarily a place where people go to die.

It is impossible for the unconscious mind to conceive of death of the self. I can understand death coming to others, but not to me. Mental defense mechanisms such as unconscious denial refuse to allow contemplation of the reality of *my* death, or of *my* body lying forever in a box underground or being burned to ashes. Others, yes, but not *me*. However, when the last few days of life arrive, most patients *know* they are dying. If doctors, nurses, and family keep denying the reality of imminent death, the patients cannot talk about it. It is good to speak with reassurance and hope if there is any shred of reality to the remotest possibility of recovery: but once death is totally inevitable, the patient must be allowed to express his own understanding of the situation. It is *not* for doctors or family to tell a patient that he is dying; it is for them to be open to listen as the patient expresses his *own* conviction of the imminent fact. To persist in lying about eventual recovery is to deny the very thing the dying person desperately needs the most: the opportunity to talk freely and honestly about anything that comes into his mind with loved ones who care, and who are not emotionally separated by pretense, deceit, or denial.

There are three things in connection with death which should be considered by everyone long before it happens. First is the donation of parts of one's body for the benefit of others, or for medical research. The cornea of a healthy eye can give sight to a partially blind person after the donor's death. Many other parts of the body, if previously bequeathed by the individual, can be used through modern surgery to bring health back to recipients suffering or even dying from defective organs. Whole bodies are always needed by medical schools for dissection and the teaching of anatomy. Second is the question of burial versus cremation. Many fundamental Bible students prefer not to be cremated on the grounds that the body, the temple of the Holy Spirit while alive, will literally be raised again at the Second Coming of Christ. Other, equally devout Christians, in the light of space availability, population increase, and personal aesthetic, ecologic and hygienic principles would prefer cremation, after which the ashes are either buried or scattered. Either way, ". . . the dead in Christ shall rise first" (1 Thessalonians 4:16) and God's statement to Adam is fulfilled: "In the sweat of thy face shalt thou eat bread, till thou return unto the ground; for out of it wast thou taken: for dust thou art, and unto dust shalt thou return" (Genesis 3:19). Third is the obligation to make a will. It does not cost much, it ensures the carrying out of one's wishes after death, and, most important, it saves one's survivors an awful lot of headaches and legal hassling.

Doctor Elisabeth Kübler-Ross in her important book *On Death and Dying* distinguishes five stages between a person's first awareness of serious fatal illness and his death. The first is *denial,* which can be either brief or last several months depending on the rapidity of the disease process. The patient says, "No, not me." This is usually followed by the stage of *anger,* during which the patient becomes critical, demanding, and difficult to talk with. He is now saying, "Why me?" Next comes the stage of *bargaining,* usually with God: "Give me another year and I will . . . ." and "Yes, me . . . but . . . ." Lapsed Christians at this stage often have a recovery of faith. Fourth is the stage of *depression* or grief when mourning and weeping occurs. "Yes, me," the patient is finally able to say, but the reality is overshadowed by the preparatory grief of impending loss, not of *a* loved one but of *all* loved ones, by his own permanent departure. Crying, even for a man, is usual at this stage, and friends and family should not feel uncomfortable but be understanding of the normality of it. The final stage is that of *acceptance.* "Yes, me . . . and it's OK." This is not the same as resignation, which would be like giving up in defeat. Acceptance can be victorious because fear has disappeared and peace comes.

Doctor Kübler-Ross states that dying is easier for those of profound personal religious faith. No dying is easy, but some people have the additional help of whatever may be the resources of their belief system. The Bible clearly teaches that those who die without having made their peace with God go to a lost eternity outside of God's presence. Even on one's deathbed it is not too late to repent of all the sins of a lifetime and to surrender to Jesus as personal Saviour and Lord. The dying sinner may feel that it is cowardly to crave forgiveness at the last minute. But God sees it differently. He is ". . . not willing that any should perish, but that all should come to repentance" (2 Peter 3:9). It is His will for ". . . all men to be saved, and to come unto the knowledge of the truth" (1 Timothy 2:4). God instantly and eternally forgives the repentant and dying sinner and gives him inner peace and strength to face imminent death. The newborn Christian then has at least three additional resources to sustain him in his last hours.

First: he knows that ". . . all things work together for good to them that love God, to them who are the called according to his purpose" (Romans 8:28). He can therefore trust that nothing ever happens to him outside of God's executive or permissive will. He can triumph with Job and cry out, "Though he slay me, yet will I trust in him" (*see* Job 13:15). He will only die when God is ready for him.

Second: the dying Christian has the comfort of the Holy Spirit to strengthen, sustain, and uphold him. He also has the conscious awareness of his intimate closeness to Jesus his Saviour, into whose eternal presence he is about to step. In that moment he can say with the hymnist, William R. Featherston:

> I'll love Thee in life, I will love Thee in death,
> And praise Thee as long as Thou lendest me breath;
> And say when the death-dew lies cold on my brow:
> If ever I loved Thee, my Jesus, 'tis now.
>
> In mansions of glory and endless delight,
> I'll ever adore Thee in heaven so bright;

> I'll sing with the glittering crown on my brow:
> If ever I loved Thee, my Jesus, 'tis now.

Finally, the Christian has the resource of his belief in immortality. A baby still in his mother's womb has no understanding of the expanded experiences of life awaiting him after birth. Likewise, God has given to us only the faintest suggestions of the reality of eternity to be spent serving Him in His infinite and glorious Creation. My personal concept of eternity is influenced by an amateur fascination with the incredible facts of astronomy. I conceptualize heaven as the infinity of all Creation in which my spirit can serve God forever. Our finite minds cannot comprehend the vastness of this Creation in which eternity is to be spent. The as-yet *unknown* Creation that lies beyond the known facts defies our comprehension, but thrills the imagination of those who believe that one day we will see and understand it.

There is no way, with present scientific knowledge, that astronauts could escape our solar system and then return to their families. Human life-span is far too short. But God makes such travel possible in the spirit because it will be outside the restrictions of space and time. In our glorified bodies we will be able to do God's bidding in both the material universe and the spiritual realm of His heavenly Kingdom. "For now we see through a glass, darkly; but then face to face: now I know in part; but then shall I know even as also I am known" (1 Corinthians 13:12).

John said: ". . . we shall be like him; for we shall see him as he is" (1 John 3:2). At the very end of the Bible he also wrote:

> And I heard a great voice out of heaven saying, Behold, the tabernacle of God is with men, and he will dwell with them, and they shall be his people, and God himself shall be with them, and be their God. And God shall wipe away all tears from their eyes; and there shall be no more death, neither sorrow, nor crying, neither shall there be any more pain: for the former things are passed away. And he that sat upon the throne said, Behold, I make all things new. . . .
>
> Revelation 21:3–5

SUGGESTED READING

Aaron, William. *Straight*. New York: Doubleday & Co., 1972.

Adams, Jay. *The Christian Counselor's Manual*. Grand Rapids, Michigan: Baker Book House, 1974.

Bird, Lewis P. and Reilly, Christopher T. *Learning to Love*. Waco, Texas: Word, Inc., 1971.

Bower, Robert K. *Solving Problems in Marriage*. Grand Rapids, Michigan: William B. Eerdmans Publishing Co., 1972.

Cole, William Graham. *Sex and Love in the Bible*. New York: Association Press, 1959.

Dobson, James. *Dare to Discipline*. Wheaton, Illinois: Tyndale House Publishers, 1971.

Drakeford, John. *Forbidden Love*. Waco, Texas: Word, Inc., 1971.

Emerson, James G. *Divorce, the Church and Remarriage*. Philadelphia: Westminster Press, 1961.

Ginott, Haim. *Between Parent and Teenager*. New York: Avon Books, 1973.

Hyder, O. Quentin. *The Christian's Handbook of Psychiatry*. Old Tappan, N.J.: Fleming H. Revell Co., 1971.

Kolb, Lawrence C., ed. *Noyes' Modern Clinical Psychiatry*. Philadelphia: W. B. Saunders Co., 1968.

Kübler-Ross, Elisabeth. *On Death and Dying*. New York: Macmillan Co., 1970.

LaHaye, Tim. *Transformed Temperaments*. Wheaton, Illinois: Tyndale House Publishers, 1971.

Lovett, C. S. *Unequally Yoked Wives*. Baldwin Park, California: Personal Christianity.

191

Mace, David R. *Sexual Difficulties in Marriage.* Philadelphia: Fortress Press, 1972.

Mallory, James D., Jr. *The Kink and I.* Grand Rapids, Michigan: Zondervan Publishing House, 1965.

Masters, William H. and Johnson, Virginia E. *The Pleasure Bond.* Boston: Little, Brown & Co., 1975.

Menninger, Karl. *Whatever Became of Sin?* New York: Hawthorn Books, 1973.

Morison, Frank. *Who Moved the Stone?* Grand Rapids, Michigan: Zondervan Publishing House.

Narramore, Bruce. *Help I'm a Parent.* Grand Rapids, Michigan: Zondervan Publishing House, 1972.

Narramore, Clyde. *Encyclopedia of Psychological Problems.* Grand Rapids, Michigan: Zondervan Publishing House, 1966.

Nelson, Marion H. *Why Christians Crack Up.* Chicago: Moody Press, 1967.

Olford, Stephen F. and Laws, Frank A. *The Sanctity of Sex.* Old Tappan, N.J.: Fleming H. Revell Co., 1963.

Payne, Dorothy. *Women Without Men.* Philadelphia: United Church Press, 1969.

Petersen, J. Allen. *For Men Only.* Wheaton, Illinois: Tyndale House Publishers, 1973.

Salk, Lee. *What Every Child Would Like His Parents to Know.* New York: David McKay Co., Inc., 1972.

Skinner, Tom. *If Christ Is the Answer, What Are the Questions.* Grand Rapids, Michigan: Zondervan Publishing House, 1966.

Stott, John R. W. *Basic Christianity.* Downers Grove, Illinois: Inter-Varsity Press, 1970.

Tournier, Paul. *A Doctor's Casebook in the Light of the Bible.* New York: Harper & Row, 1960.

Van De Velde, Theodoor H. *Ideal Marriage.* New York: Random House, 1965.

Vincent, Merville O. *God Sex and You.* Philadelphia: J. B. Lippincott Co., 1971.

Wagner, Maurice E. *Put It All Together.* Grand Rapids, Michigan: Zondervan Publishing House, 1974.